Table o

Introduction

It has been said that the longest twelve inches on Earth is the distance between the head and the heart. This book is my personal testament to that potent little understatement. It is a story of profound, personal awakening. Autobiographical in nature, it is a timeline that, in hindsight, makes perfect sense to me only now. Looking back, it's easy to see how so many events dovetailed together and that each step was not only necessary, but even likely imminent.

This book is about three different lives of mine. Not as in past lifetimes, but three portions of this life. For that reason, I have divided this book into three sections. You will see that in my first life, I did not believe in anything esoteric, or what I used to condescendingly categorize as mystical garbage. I now write about many of these things because I have experienced them for myself. This is a true story of a left-brained, rational thinking person, and how I learned, after several decades, to get out of my head. I have been instructed by a Voice whose very existence I denied for decades, to get this story of awakening into our planet's collective consciousness.

The Voice, which I now understand to be my Soul or Higher Self, took me on a most uncomfortable adventure out of my rational mind and more toward my heart. For over twenty years, my rational mind grudgingly rolled my eyes at all things mystical or esoteric. I now see them differently because I have, thankfully, experienced many of these things first hand. I didn't believe it. I do now.

I hope to, in turn, inspire you to listen to your Voice within. The Voice that is always, and has always been there. If we can listen well enough, it can protect us from things we do not necessarily need to endure – yet the key word here is necessary. I now believe that there are sometimes things that do indeed need to be endured. Along my journey, I have fallen deeply in love with all parts of yoga, and a quote from the late beloved yogi and mystic B.K.S. Iyengar speaks to this. He said, "Yoga teaches us to cure what need not be endured and to endure what cannot be cured." Yes, yoga and my story here has taught me this.

I fully believe that we come into the physical body still connected to spirit, and it gets rationalized out of us. Yet even before the rationalization starts to take place, we come into these human bodies having forgotten who we truly are. Furthermore, I believe (and there are copious amounts of evidence for this) that it is by design. It is called the forgetting process, or the veiling process. Briefly, this is the process every single person goes through as they are born. The conscious mind is separated from the unconscious mind, which is

2

always connected to spirit. Having forgotten the One, Source, God, Spirit, or however you personally define it, we have no choice but to live on faith. At a certain point in my first life, I concluded that the notion of faith was a crutch for people who did not want to understand. I now see that this is what my head wanted. Thanks to the experiences that you will read about, I was transformed into my second life. Along the way, I learned that faith is in the heart, not in the head. Over the past twenty years, it has been clinically proven that the heart has an intelligence.[1] One could say that I had to learn it the "heart" way, though.

Since there is no book or testimony that could convince the skeptic, I ask the reader to consider this book to be the story of this skeptic's utter surprise upon finding the world of woo-woo to be very real. After scoffing at such things for over two decades, I now stand corrected. When I told my friend Toby I was learning about all sorts of esoteric things, she said to me, "You're not learning. You're remembering."

Mine is only one story of a growing number of us who have had an enormous spiritual awakening since 2012. The Mayan calendar and other ancient prophecies pointed at 2012 being the end of something. There are always those who assume the

---

[1] "Research Library." HeartMath Institute. https://www.heartmath.org/research/research-library/.

gloom and doom, believing these to foretell the end of the world. Does 2012 mean something? I didn't believe so in 2012, but I do now. But the end of what, exactly? The end of the world? I do not think so. I would now say that it was the beginning of the end of the world as we know it. I have thought of myself as spiritual and philosophical my entire life, even as a child. Yet a whole new world has been revealed to me. If this book holds your attention, you may recognize a similar journey you have been on or are currently being guided through.

This is a true story of me forgetting so much that I joined in what some might refer to as an atheistic cult for almost twenty-three years. But it couldn't have happened any other way because the rewards were all the sweeter. When my lessons were over in the organization, the Voice led me to my graduation, and the celebration continues today as I progress through the post-grad school of being in the physical while once again reconnecting to spirit. My mind has been beautifully blown, and I am remembering.

My personal story here proposes that we can release every last form of judging things to be good or bad in one's life. On the Soul level, all things are good. As I write this paragraph it is January 2018, and it's been a pretty crazy couple of years. We have seen Facebook fights and people unfriending one another over politics. We saw arm waving, clenched-fist politicians, mass shootings, and throngs of people protesting police brutality. Earthquakes, floods, and broken economies across the world remind us of apocalyptic prophecies from ancient scripture. At the end of my first life, however; I learned that the world is only how we view it. From the spiritual standpoint, I hope to illustrate why I believe it's all good.

So in a blissful state and with watery eyes, I sit at my keyboard in gratitude and in awe. Gratitude to the Voice. Humbled by the Dark Night of the Soul, from which I eventually recognized the light, even if it took what felt like centuries at the time. I express here all of my gratitude for confusion and obstacles, as I believe that all obstacles are a catalyst for growth if we can recognize them. As I finish this sentence, Freddy (one of my two cats who are brothers) starts his usual parading back and forth in front of my computer monitor, impeding my writing progress. As he offers his affectionate head butts, I am reminded of the twelve-inch journey where, with our heads gently touching, I am in my heart in this moment. There are countless little things to enjoy in this life, and there are so many little things that slow us down while we are trying to accomplish something the left-brain wants to complete. Trying to write a book while having a cat sashaying in front of my computer monitor is one of those opportunities to just slow down. That's when the

Voice can be heard. Thank you, Freddy.

For the reader who sees things in the world as right or wrong, this book is an admission of my having been wrong. For the reader who believes that everything is in divine order, this book is about my coming home. I will say that I have made up for lost time in my studies of the topics at which I once rolled my eyes – but I now know that I am not learning about these concepts. I am indeed remembering.

Note: Some names in this book will be changed in order to protect privacy.

Section 1

Chapter 1
Earliest Memories

I was born in San Antonio, Texas, on June 21, 1958 at 6:32 p.m. smack dab in the middle of the "cuspiest-cusp" between Cancer and Gemini. I was the first child of a twenty-two-year-old father (who was the youngest of three and freshly out of the Air Force) and a creative, emotionally charged mother who was the eldest of six. Due to being born in the Great Depression (or just after in the case of my mother) they were both humble, hard working, and kind Mid-westerners. My father's mother had brought her family to Kansas City from tiny West Plains, Missouri, where she had been running a local tavern. She removed my father from school in the eighth grade so he could help support the family. As a boy, he would have preferred to stay in school as well as West Plains. My mother's family was from KC, and my parents met at the El Torian Skating Rink around 1956 when all buildings' architecture, even warehouses and roller skating rinks, had a purpose. One of my earliest memories is seeing my father spinning on one skate, seated on one foot, while extending his other leg.

My parents divorced when I was four, but not before bringing my younger sister, Ann, into the physical. My mother immediately remarried one of the two sons of the owners of the neighborhood bakery. I don't consciously remember many events in those years of my life, but I do vaguely remember a scene in the divorce court and my mom being rather happy as we got in the car to leave the court. I remember my grandmother (on my mother's side) pinning one of those old worn out, paper-thin Fifties' terrycloth towels to the back of my shirt so that I could run down the hill of her huge front yard and pretend to be Superman while looking back over my shoulder to see the towel flapping in the wind just like it did on TV in the old series. The few other memories are limited to my Tonka Truck, a Jack in the box, and that I got a Huckleberry Hound cake on my fourth birthday.

The first pivotal event I remember happening to me was when I was three or four years old. I believe it was while my parents were separated, or it might have been just before that. Our modest house was on the corner, so we had a large side yard. There was a tree that grew only inches from the house which, in hindsight, most people would have plucked up as a sapling since it would eventually disrupt the cement slab of the 1954 tract home. I still have dreams about that home sometimes. I believe that, on a subconscious level, I consider that house to be my true home.

One sunny summer day, there was a boy about my age who lived in the house caddy-cornered from ours. He came over into our yard where I was playing with a toy rifle of mine. He took my rifle and in perfect alignment with all other thieves with guns, ran back to his house. Confused, I went inside and told my mother about the strange event that I did not understand. She took me across the street, and we confronted the boy who was, of course, accompanied by his mother about the theft. He denied taking my prized rifle, and it's not surprising that his mother believed him. I can still visualize the scene with our house to my left side and the aforementioned tree above me as I looked up at my mother pointing toward the house on the opposite corner.

Newly introduced to theft and deceit, I started my journey from the heart to the head, otherwise known as rational thinking. *Why would he take my rifle? How could his mother not believe me?* Questions like these started me on what would eventually be many years of thunderstorms filled with "whys" and "hows." I clearly remember thinking that the theft and the lie were interesting even if it didn't feel just. I suppose other kids may discover what a lie is from the other side of the fence, by learning they can manipulate others by not telling the truth. This was my introduction. I was not angry nor sad. I was more fascinated than anything else. That event set me on a course for justice and truth, both of which I would be heavily involved with later in life.

I became more deeply drawn toward integrity as the years went on. These ideals would be reinforced by the actions of my father, and I would grow to learn he had a great deal of integrity. He always kept his word, no matter what. Of course, my mother contributed to my passion for truth and justice, like the old superman show said, by insisting her kids tell the truth when asked which of us had broken something or made a mess. (I am still the world's worst liar.) Wanting to champion truth as a kid also happened to mean I was an excellent tattle-tale. Wanting to champion truth in my teens and twenties, I had endless philosophical debates. Wanting to champion truth later in my thirties, I joined an organization that supported human rights and protested the many injustices on the planet. I believed I was doing necessary work for the world; I have since discovered the necessary work that was happening inside of me as I got close to truly remembering.

As early as I can remember, I tried to make people laugh. I inherently know that I developed this talent as a way to lighten the vibe of the home of parents going through a divorce. My mother and the entire side of her family have a stellar sense of humor, and I was blessed to have been raised with this as it served me well throughout my life. My mother recounts many stories of me deliberately making people laugh. Many other people who grew up to be performers had similar itches to scratch as children, and this skill set me up to be the class clown in school.

Money was in short supply in both homes even though my dad did a wonderful job of not showing it. I recently saw an old piece of paper he had taped to the inside of a closet door which had a chart of all of his bills listed. He used a ruler to make around fifteen categories, where he would methodically check each box as the bill was paid. Child support wasn't even on the list because that was always on time, no matter what. As I did the math, I was completely overcome with emotion realizing just how dedicated he was to supporting us while making so little. This kind, gentle, humble man still nurtures today at eighty-two years old every time he wobbles to the back door of his small house and tosses peanuts and bird seed out on the patio with a tin roof for the assorted squirrels, birds, and chipmunks who have learned they can depend on his kindness to survive the cold KC winters. He has even placed a deck box on the patio with pet doors as well as heaters for any strays. This is the kindness I was raised in.

Chapter 2
Forgiveness and Forgetting

As we go into this chapter, I would like to
clearly say that none of the things you read here about
from my childhood are meant to elicit sympathy. I
believe my life has actually been a cakewalk compared
to most. Many of us grow up in what we might think
of as less-than-perfect circumstances, yet I have found
this is not really the case. If our walk is not
challenging, we learn nothing. If the weight is not
heavy, we will not grow stronger. Mine has likely been
an easier path, and I now understand why. I am most
grateful for the events that have formed the person
sitting here today. Your story is quite possibly more
interesting than mine. If there is one wish I have in
writing down my story, it's that you might remember
events in your life and find that your story has a happy
ending. There are no unhappy endings.

Maybe the biggest lesson from my childhood,
which I know was no accident, was the lesson of
forgiveness. As mentioned, my mother remarried. Let's
just say I was not his biggest fan. He was quite short
tempered, but as I learned later in my life, his mother
was dominating and manipulative to most everyone,
including her family. In spite of his mother being so
callous, she eventually outlived him by about twenty
years.

My stepdad would occasionally joke around with me, so I could tell that liked me. However, he had stern rules, and his short temper would flare up for the smallest of infractions. He inherited that nastiness from his mother, and that short temper would eventually lurk its way into my personality as I got older. I was afraid of him and of my mother for allowing him to strike us so often. I don't wish to give you the idea that we were constantly beaten, but it was far more than necessary, and I knew it back then. I understand both sides of the corporeal punishment discussion, so I'll simply say that what makes me writhe is an adult striking a child in anger, and that was the case with us.

Largely due to this, Ann and I wanted to live with my dad full-time instead of only on weekends. We continued to have that dream as we grew, and I knew very well back then that she struggled with it more than I did. I was the oldest. I had to be strong. Besides, I knew inside that I was just biding my time. I had gone into my rational mind again and understood that the situation was temporary. I knew I would be free from all of it eventually, but I was never able to help Ann understand this. My father's home gave me enough love to get me through the week, which I calculated (in my rational head) as 168 hours. Wednesday at noon was the exact halfway point to reach Fridays, the day my dad would pick us up for the weekend.

It's not uncommon in divorced homes that one ex will complain of the other. This was the case for my mother. One day in the basement laundry room, she was in the middle of another mini-rant about my dad. I could physically feel her, as well as myself, shrinking and contracting in that energy of complaining. Then it hit me. I rationally understood, emotionally understood, and could even physically feel that forgiveness was not for the one being forgiven. It was for the one doing the forgiving. What a wonderful realization this was at the age of eight. It was putting me on the road to inherently knowing a crucial truth: There is nothing to forgive.

While my mother may have been able to hold a grudge, she was also sensitive and creative as well. She had me help her with her pottery, framing of her poetry, cooking, and any other project she was working on. She passionately loved music and was a fine singer herself. My alarm clock every morning while she was getting ready for work was Roberta Flack, Jethro Tull, Joe Cocker, Traffic, The Spinners, Kiss, Lou Rawls, and so many more. Music would incorporate into my waking dreams. It's no surprise that I was drawn to be a musician and singer myself, and it provided for me quite well in Las Vegas for thirty years.

Although my mother had complained about him, my father never spoke an ill word about her. His silence is a testament to his integrity, which I bathed in two days a week as a child. He had fought hard to win weekend custody of Ann and me. That was not always an easy feat in the early Sixties. He was the best father I can imagine having, and today my mother agrees wholeheartedly. He blessed my life with balance in his different ways of parenting compared to my mother and stepfather. He would pick us up at 6 p.m. every Friday and bring us back (sadly for Ann and me at the time) at 6 p.m. on Sundays. My stepdad was the kind of man, who, born from mean stock, would not let us go out the front door on Fridays until precisely 6 p.m. In other words, if my dad was five minutes early, we would need to wait those five minutes.

As a single father in the Sixties, he thought it wise to take us to church so that my mother and stepfather would not have any leverage against his already tenuous weekend custody rights. He found the LDS religion to be acceptable, though he left the church a few years later after asking questions they could not answer. Being a seeker, he had books on UFOs, Astral Travel, etc. My father was (and still is) a curious man, and I definitely didn't fall far from the tree.

As we joyfully jumped in his car for the weekend, my dad would ask how our week was. Since I had learned that forgiveness was the best policy for my inner harmony, I would reply that the week was good. Ann, still unaware of the prized gem of forgiveness I had discovered, would retort to the contrary and go on to explain what our mother and stepfather had done that week. Not surprisingly, this would upset my father and make for a rougher than preferred start to our forty-eight hours together, and we lived for those two days every week. Ann was amazingly strong in those years, and she still is. She was almost defiant of what we felt at the time was, my mother's and stepfather's iron-fist rule. She would not let her spirit be broken, and as a result she endured even more of the physical retribution than I did. She took a different path where resistance would be her form of integrity. While I was afraid, she defied. I had figured out how to play the game and keep the peace.

Ann often bruised from the strikes, and my father once took photos of the bruises and contacted an attorney. That's when he gained control of the custody situation. With the photos, my father most likely could have won full-time custody, but he did not want us to grow up without a mother. This showed his integrity even more. He did, however, draw clear boundaries with her.

Part of the new boundaries included receiving us for two weeks every summer when we would go on vacations out west. Attending the LDS church for those few years meant we would stop in Salt Lake City to see the temple. I loved eating cheeseburgers for every meal. My father and Ann would have to wait longer for our order because I was a ketchup-only kid. The smell of chlorine from the motel pools still reminds me of those vacations when I would run back to the room, teeth chattering upon hitting the air conditioning.

While I might find the drive long and uneventful now, the 500 mile trek west across Kansas and eastern Colorado was the adventure of a lifetime for me as a kid. I had also known by the age of eight that I wanted to leave where I was living, and the first vacation was my practice run. Toward the end of that leg of the drive, I saw what looked to be some sort of huge clouds in the distance. I asked my dad what they were, and he told me I was seeing the mountains. I couldn't believe it. I had never dreamed mountains were so big. Headed back east, we would loop around and take the southern route where I had the same awestruck reaction to the deserts of Utah, Arizona, and New Mexico. The desert called to me for some reason. It reminded me of the bottom of an ocean without the water. At this point in my life, I now have the feeling that upon seeing these places, I was feeling a strong connection to another life as a Native American in the desert, though I have only recently begun to entertain that idea. The desert skies, the monuments made of red rocks, and the Grand Canyon all called to me as if they were home. Maybe they were.

My plans for my departure were only fueled every time I saw one of the Sixties' Westerns or California beach movies. I didn't feel comfortable where I was living. It smelled of bigotry and racism. I clearly recall an incident that introduced me to these things. My stepfather was picking up some supplies for his family's bakery in downtown KC. Ann and I were in the back of his '57 Chevy which was parked in front of the supply store, and I saw a black man walking on the sidewalk.

"Look mommy, a N*****!" I exclaimed. They immediately turned to me.

"Shhh! Don't say that!" they both hissed. I didn't understand why they were telling me to be quiet. Why couldn't I say this word? Any parent knows that children repeat what they hear their parents say, and I had heard my stepfather say the N-word often.

I grew to feel an increasing alienation from

what I was learning on earth as a child. I would often look out my window at night at the stars and the moon and ask myself, *Why am I here? How did we all get here?* I felt some sort of deep connection to the stars. I loved Sci-Fi shows like *Star Trek* and *Lost in Space.* I was fascinated by the vastness of the universe. I didn't know why. I just knew there was a connection, a fascination with the infinite.

Chapter 3
Into my Teens

When I was fourteen, my mother divorced my stepdad. This obviously came as a welcome surprise for me. However, it crushed my stepsister (his only child), who would have been eight at that time. I started to realize that she had always been, in a way, on her own in that family. Until that time, she had not known what it was like to be a part of a broken family. While she had the love of her father and mother, she was, in a way, an only child since my sister and I never bonded with her father. My sister and I still had our family, though broken. Unfortunately for my stepsister, her family became broken as well.

My mother soon started dating a man around eight years her junior named Paul. He was only ten years older than me. Paul was a muscular guy, sweet to my mom, and nice to us kids. He had a yellow Pontiac LeMans with an eight-track tape player that introduced me to Buffalo Springfield, a musical group I fell in love with. I remember stealing a good amount of nickels and dimes from his huge spare change jar, and I have always felt guilty for it. (I apologize for that, Paul. I owe you about ten dollars.)

Ann continued to be a challenge for my mom after Paul entered the picture. Her pattern was already ingrained. My mom finally had enough of Ann's defiant behavior and told my dad that he would have to take Ann. She and I had always wanted to live with him, and I thought, *Wait a minute. I always behave, tell the truth and do everything I'm asked, and she gets to move in with dad?* I am still not exactly sure of the turn of events, but I assume my dad said something similar to my mother. Paul and my mother realized it as well, so I was given the choice of where I would live. I finally moved in with my dad. I was incredibly happy, despite my mom being disappointed that I chose to leave her home. But for me, it had always been the plan. I was just paying my dues until the right time.

I was living where I wanted and had reached my stride in my self-confidence. I finished my sophomore year at the new school. That summer was glorious because I didn't have to wash clothes, scrub floors, or pull weeds. I now understand the importance of doing all those things, but to a fourteen year old, I was living the life. I had a small motorcycle and friends I would go riding with. There were hills, trails, streams, and a million trees on a huge piece of land where people had been riding for years. The trick was making sure we didn't get caught riding on the streets going to and coming from "The Trails" as we called them.

One day that summer, I saw my ex-stepfather driving by my dad's house. I understood that he had purposely driven by just to see if I would be in sight. I also understood then that he missed me. I waved, and he pulled the van over. We exchanged a few words. I had no animosity toward him whatsoever. While living with him, I was afraid of him, but I had nothing but compassion for him in that moment. I knew he must have been in pain, and for the first time, I saw that he had loved me.

At seventeen, I started experimenting with drugs. I was a part-timer with LSD and mushrooms, and I had only absolutely beautiful experiences with those. I felt at home when experiencing them. I knew the oneness with the planet and the universe, and I recall literally feeling the Earth move while standing out in the forest one night. Not very long after graduating from High School, I followed my best friend to Dallas. There was also a new addition to my experimenting with drugs: cocaine.

Chapter 4
The Rocky Road

That year while living in Dallas, I was out with my friends and we had just picked up a gram of cocaine from someone's apartment. I also had a small amount of pot in a rolled-up baggie. I believe that the police were watching that person's apartment because as soon as we all got into my friend's car and he put it in drive, the police pulled us over. I quickly stuffed the envelope, the "snow seal" of cocaine into my left shoe in order to conceal it. When I did that, however; I inadvertently let the cuff of my left pant leg get caught up over the rolled-up baggie of pot which was stuffed in my left sock. An officer came up to the driver's side, and another officer came to the passenger side where I was sitting. Of course, they were asking if we had anything illegal on us. The officer on my side shined his flashlight into the car.

"Looks like this guy's going to jail tonight!" he said when he saw the baggie I had overlooked. I was so concerned about the cocaine that I didn't even make sure the pot was out of sight. My heart was pounding. I had never been busted before. It was bad enough to be arrested for pot in Texas at that time. The cocaine, however, was a far more serious matter, and I knew it.

The police took me to the old Dallas county jail,

and given their "redneckness," I think they did that purposefully to scare me. It worked. He had the southern accent and the "don't mess with Texas" attitude. The officer who was so happy he found my baggie of pot was sitting next to me in the back seat the entire ride to the jail.

"Boy, you got anything else illegal on you?" he kept asking me. "You'd better tell me now because if I find anything when I strip search you, I'm gonna make it as hard on you as I can."

I kept shaking my head "no" all the while knowing he would find the cocaine in my shoe. I was terrified. What felt like my funeral procession to the jail finally ended where I was strip searched as promised. He looked through all my pockets, looked in a rather private area, and I knew the shoes were next. I was counting the seconds until my life would be over. He turned my right shoe upside down, and it was empty. Then the dreaded left shoe. He tapped it to release the envelope that would end my life. Then it happened – the snow seal envelope somehow caught on the arch of my shoe and did not fall out. I spent the night in jail knowing something extraordinary had happened.

I soon decided that I'd had enough of Texas and moved back to KC, touting my good fortune with the

Dallas police to all my friends. My narrow escape was a good story for all who partook in illegal substances. Feeling indestructible (as teens tend to feel, but even more so after the Dallas police matter), I went further down the rabbit hole. Within a year, I was nineteen and somehow had become an IV cocaine user. I was, however, a fully functioning IV user and held down a great job at a progressive convenience store chain. One of the things I enjoyed most was working with the public. I loved the job and worked for the company for about four years, all the while hiding my shadow side to all but one, a very kind and sensitive friend named John who also worked for the company.

It was a crazy, polarized life. I was in my early twenties, successful in an intimate, public face-to-face business world, yet living this vastly darker life of IV cocaine use off the clock. I felt tremendous guilt for not being able to quit. I was happier at work while making people laugh, yet I knew what was coming. It was like the Bowie song from those years, "Ashes to Ashes," which is about IV drug use. "I'm stuck with a valuable friend," and, "We know major Tom's a junkie," were among the lyrics. The later it got in the day, the more guilt would arrive as I knew my evening fate. I would drive home while consuming the first of about ten beers for the evening in order to rush back to my "valuable friend." Like a ghoul, the deep-seated guilt would start to creep in again at the end of the night when I had no more cocaine and knew I would get little sleep before having to get up and go to work. The guilt completely consumed me.

Chapter 5
Getting Out

In April of 1983, I was twenty-four and quite tired of the work-cocaine-work-cocaine grind. I received a call from a close friend from high school. He was a great keyboard player/singer and had been in a band playing on the road for a year or two. He said they were putting a new band together and asked if I would like to drive to St. Louis to audition for the band. None of the other guys in that band knew me, so an audition was needed. I dreamed and prayed that this might be my ticket out of Kansas City, and especially away from the drug monkey on my back. I thought that if I left town, I would have a better chance of leaving my addiction behind. I passed the audition. I immediately gave my two-week notice at my job and headed back to St. Louis to begin rehearsing. I envisioned a new life out west in California where the band had planned to settle. I would be in an L.A. band! We rehearsed for eight weeks and headed west to seek our fortune. Thanks to leaving my fellow druggies in KC, I had gotten away from the IV use, though I did still occasionally use cocaine. One step at a time, I figured. As when in Dallas, I once again lucked my way out. And, I was finally leaving KC.

We played all over the Southwest, and I loved it. I was again seeing the mountains and the deserts I had loved so much when on vacations with Ann and my dad. The desert skies of Arizona were boundless. I swam in the crystal clear Colorado River. I saw majestic desert sunsets. I was living my dream of playing music. I even went through twenty-five bottles of beer on my twenty-fifth birthday. Yep, still pushing it at the time.

I grew accustomed to having my entire life in my car since we traveled so much. Living in Los Angeles and being the trusting Midwesterner I was, forgot to lock my car while at the movie, and my guitar was stolen. Just as when my toy rifle was stolen twenty years earlier, I wasn't angry. I got it. Some people steal. The Voice was telling me, *There is nothing to forgive.* I figured that if there was a mistake made, it was mine for not having locked my car. I definitely needed a new guitar, though. I found the guitar I would buy in the Thrifty Nickel flier. I drove out to look at it, and it came home with me that night.

A few days later, I was admiring the beautiful paint job on my new guitar. Someone had done some subtle art work on it, but I had not seen it the night I bought it. It was faint, but it was there. I had to get just the right angle in the light to see it. There was the outline of an exactly-to-scale right hand. It looked like when you make the shape of a gun using your right hand before the hammer comes down. The hand was pointing at something. I had to tilt the guitar again in order to see the approximately two inch object being pointed to. It was the normal Christian image of...the devil? A devil with all of the usual trappings: a tail, horns, and a pitchfork. As I looked even closer, I could see that this devil was holding something else. It was a type of banner or scroll that quoted Revelations 20:10, which reads:

And the devil that deceived them was cast into the lake of fire and brimstone, where the beast and the false prophet are, and shall be tormented day and night for ever and ever.[2]

I definitely thought that this guitar was more than a coincidence. I was wondering why it made its way into my hands, but I didn't go nearly as far as thinking that it was necessary for my other guitar to have been stolen in order for it to find me.

While I found the whole event more than coincidental, things got more interesting. A couple of days later, I noticed something else in that image, on the back of the hand which was pointing at the devil. It was a scar on the back of the hand. And guess what was on the back of my hand? You guessed it. A scar that was an exact match. The length, width and proportions were precisely the same. I could literally

---

[2] Rev. 20:10 KJ21

place my hand over the image and replace it perfectly. It was truly as if someone traced my right hand, including the scar, and faintly impressed the image under the thick lacquer of the guitar. I felt this could not be a coincidence but had no way of understanding why or how this guitar was sent to me. Like the Dallas jail story, I was just content showing it off to people how that hand and my hand were exactly the same size. The scar was from when I burned the top of my hand on an electric oven while still in KC about two years earlier. It has since faded so that only the slightest hint remains. As the years went on, I pretty much forgot about the whole thing and kept enjoying my continued good luck.

Chapter 6
Vegas Bound

By spring of 1985, the band leader's wife had convinced him to dissolve the band. (This hardly ever happens, of course. Musicians will get this joke.) I had given up on making a living at music in Los Angeles due to the cost of living as well as an overabundance of talent and a deficiency of venues to play. That city has a reputation for chewing up aspiring artists as a wood chipper does to the stoutest of limbs, spitting us out in pieces to another location. Not wanting to go back to Kansas City, I decided to try Las Vegas. I had kind of laughed at the idea of Las Vegas entertainment and wanted to be a "real musician" and stay in Los Angeles where all the big boys were. Since I didn't have any success in Los Angeles, I thought Las Vegas was my only option. It was a last resort because I knew going back to Kansas City would be the end of me, where I knew I would reunite with my old "valuable friends."

My dad sent me $600 to rent an apartment in Las Vegas. It wasn't the first or last time he would do that in those years. Within a couple of months, I found a successful band to play with. This was a popular act, and we worked pretty much anywhere we wanted. The leader, Chris, was quite talented and had a good head for business. Her drive was amazing as well as having the passion for performing which continues today some thirty-five years later. We rehearsed two days a week whether we needed it or not (said with a hint of sarcasm) and we were renown in Las Vegas.

Throughout the first six years in that band, I partied all night almost every night, only without the IV use. Though not quite as deep into the drugs as two years before, I was definitely still in over my head. Pot, moderate cocaine use (if there was such a thing), vodka, beer, and a pack of Camels every day. Don't worry, they were the filter kind. I was still partying while also working hard. My mother taught me about hard work as well as the power of music, and I was fulfilling my dream by making a living from my two passions, music and staying out of KC.

I continued my love affair with the desert climate. Midwest winters can be rough. While enjoying the Vegas music scene throughout those years, I made several life-long friends in that band. Tim was one of my band mates throughout most of the years with Chris. We are still good friends today and always enjoyed talking about what many call conspiracy theories and subjects such as the Kennedy assassination, UFOs, etc. For the record, the Kennedy assassination conspiracy theories and many more are, now, provable fact.[3] Tim and I listened to Art Bell's late night radio show. Art was the biggest contemporary pioneer in getting information that was considered by the mainstream to be occult, conspiracy, UFOs, paranormal, poltergeists, Bigfoot, etc. out to the public. If you remember Art, you know that he was always open-minded but was no fool. He was responsible for bringing information like this to millions of listeners all over the world on Sunday nights in the early 1990s. His show became so popular that he was soon on six nights a week. Art's program would eventually be hosted by George Noory, another curious interviewer who continues in Art's footsteps even today.[4] Other great hosts such as Jimmy Church and George Knapp guest host the program now as well, and today it is called Coast to Coast AM.

In some cases, the Coast to Coast listeners report they or a family member sighted a UFO. In other cases they may say they have seen an image of their deceased mother who came to them and

[3] Shenon, Philip. "Yes, the CIA Director Was Part of the JFK Assassination Cover-Up." Politico Magazine. October 06, 2015. https://www.politico.com/magazine/story/2015/10/jfk-assassination-john-mccone-warren-commission-cia-213197.
[4] "Coast to Coast AM Radio: The Latest Paranormal News." Coast to Coast AM Radio. https://www.coasttocoastam.com/.

communicated. Some may have had or heard of some paranormal experience such as a haunting or poltergeists. In many cases, like me, none of those things happened to us, but we knew that millions of people seeing the same thing probably meant there was some validity to their stories. We knew that there had to be more than what was being acknowledged by the mass media.

Coast to Coast remains an extremely popular program decades years later. People across the entire planet are thirsty for the truth. More and more people are figuring out that there is so much more than what mainstream media tells us. The reason I decided to write this book was because of what has been revealed to me, and I'm just at the tip of the iceberg. I have never really bought in to what the masses believe, yet I had no idea what I would discover years later. As my story unfolds here, you will see that what eventually manifested itself to me has taken me on, almost literally, the ride of a lifetime.

Chapter 7
Out of This World

In 1992, almost seven years after moving to Las Vegas, while playing at the Las Vegas Hilton, I met a very charismatic woman named Marie. She was traveling with a man from France who was doing a small US tour promoting his book. She was only in Las Vegas for the night. She was going to Los Angeles the next morning for another lecture. We were immediately attracted to each other. She volunteered to pay half of my plane ticket if I would like to come down and spend the day with her. I took her up on her offer. The next day, we were sitting on a park bench in Santa Monica, enjoying looking into each other's eyes and exchanging a few kisses. As we chatted, I asked her more about her reason for traveling. She told me about the man, Rael, and his book that he wrote after meeting an extraterrestrial in 1973. Having listened to Art's show meant I was no stranger to UFOs and people who claimed they had "close encounters" with them. I was also fascinated with a program called *In Search of...* hosted by the beloved Leonard Nimoy from the original Star Trek series.[5] This thought-provoking show presented mysteries such as UFOs and many other anomalies that science was thus far unable to explain. One particular thing from the

---

[5] "In Search Of Full Episodes, Video & More." History. https://www.history.com/shows/in-search-of.

show still sticks out in my mind today. What looked to be a spark plug from an internal combustion engine was found when a desert stone about the size of a softball was cut in half. I had a big appetite for things like this and it seemed obvious to me that we as a species had very little idea of the bigger picture.

I went with Marie that evening to see Rael speak. There was a short video that set up the topic of his lecture. The video was not at all professionally put together, but it made the points it was trying to get across. It was stating information about how humans and extraterrestrials had interacted throughout history. Furthermore, how ETs had created all life on earth and how they love their creation and would like to return, but they would never come uninvited. If humanity wished for them to return, we would need to invite them by building an embassy for them.

I didn't really have a strong response to the information. I was just taking it all in. And my thoughts about my new female friend were ranging from, *She's really beautiful,* to, *This might be a cult.* I stayed and listened to Rael speak. By the end of the evening, I was not deeply impressed with any of the information I had heard, even though it sounded possible. Nonetheless, I shelled out ten dollars for his book. It crossed my mind that he may have a Rolls Royce or something similar, and I was helping to gas it up for him. I spent the night with Marie, and she took me to the airport the next day to return to Las Vegas.

Two days later, I began reading Rael's book in my free time. Rael's birth name was Claude Vorillhon, but the ET he met suggested he begin to go by the name of Rael. The ET said the name means "the one who brings the light." As I began to read his book, I had to admit it was interesting. I finished the book in two days and read it again. More and more questions which I had briefly pondered over my life were being answered. Those answers brought more questions, and those would be provided by more answers. I couldn't stop thinking about all of it.

There were two people in Las Vegas who followed Rael, known as Raelians. I contacted them and happily bought Rael's other two books to devour as well. After a few weeks, I was highlighting like crazy and cross-referencing with other books. This was before the internet, and within a few weeks, Barnes and Noble and the library replaced hanging out at the casino after work.

Rael's book told his story of meeting an extraterrestrial in December of 1973. He said this ET visited him six days in a row in the crater of an extinct volcano and that the ET told him that their race, the Elohim of the Bible, had created all life on Earth. Only a couple of months earlier, I had a conversation with my friend Tim, in which he told me about the Raelians. When he said that they believe that ETs had created all life on Earth, I remember telling him that was completely bogus, and I believed in God. So here I was, eating my words and loving what I was reading. These books made a lot of sense to me, logically explaining how life appeared on Earth. Among many other things, it reconciled the idea of both a Creator of life on earth as well as UFOs and life on other planets. For me, traditional religions are far from reconciling the presence of both.

Rael said that these ETs told him that they had terraformed the Earth and created an atmosphere, microbial life, and eventually all life including their masterpiece, human beings. They said they created us scientifically through the mastery of DNA as well as with their artists who made life both beautiful, and functional. The ETs said they did not create us with a Soul, but eternal life is possible through an advanced cloning, which even Earth scientists themselves will be able to accomplish soon. Rael said the ET was quoting verse after verse of the Bible and explaining what was actually being described as opposed to what has been understood in scripture. This was more than 30 years before the History Channel program, *Ancient Aliens* came out.[6] If you're not familiar with the program, it gives a great deal of support to the idea that humanity has been visited by UFOs and ETs for thousands of years. One example given in *Ancient Aliens*, which was also given to Rael, was from the book of Ezekiel. The ET said that the opening chapter of Ezekiel's description of a "wheel within a wheel" referred to a UFO. It also explained that the star of Bethlehem was the same, both having been purposely shown to people. The ET finished with telling Rael that they would like to return but as they respect our free will, they would not come unless they were invited. The free will concept will be important when we move into the third section of this book.

Rael's books made a lot of sense to me. Since my father had *Chariots of the Gods* by Erich Von Daniken when I was a kid, the idea that a man was contacted by an ET was not a big stretch of the mind for me. It was quite possible – especially seeing Bible verses from a context of ETs "coming from the heavens" as so many verses stated about angels. I had also discovered that the word "angel" literally means "messenger." I also fully resonated with their philosophy of universal love, forgiveness, peace, and more.

---

[6] "Ancient Aliens Full Episodes, Video & More." History. https://www.history.com/shows/ancient-aliens.

Part of what the Elohim allegedly told Rael included suggestions for taking care of the human body by not partaking in drugs, smoking, or drinking hard alcohol. When my friend had called in 1983 and I joined the band, I was free from KC as well as IV drug use. This time, I answered the ET call and stopped drinking, stopped smoking cigarettes and pot, and ended my relationship with cocaine. All in one day, I was clean and sober. I started exercising regularly because I was afraid I would get fat without smoking. The changes made me feel fantastic.

My friends were surprised at my 180-degree turn. Most were supportive, yet not surprisingly, I could feel an alienation from my partying friends. It had been years of us drinking and doing cocaine all night together, often until 11 a.m. It sometimes got back to me that they were kind of rolling their eyes at my new ET story, but I didn't care. I even felt a little sorry for them that they didn't understand. Most were supportive, though, and tolerated me telling them how logical it is that ETs, who have been visiting the Earth for thousands of years, genetically created all life. I smile now knowing many of them watch *Ancient Aliens* and surely remember me telling them many of the same things back in 1992.

My dad was still in KC, but we spoke about

once a week. I told him about the book I was reading, about Rael, and what I was reading about the Elohim, UFOs, and many details in the book. His first words were, "Don't send them any money." It still makes me smile when I remember this. I sent him a copy of the book, and when I called him the next week, he said, "You're right. It does make a lot of sense." I had my second confirmation since I trusted my dad like I trust no other person on Earth. He passively supported the RM for many years. I went on to spend more and more hours actively involved in many different sides in the RM, though I eventually resigned over 20 years later. We both knew the book was a rational explanation for many things. Rational thinking comes from the head. But the reason the Voice told me to write this book is to tell the story of how I got out of my head, and into my heart.

Chapter 8
If You Are Fortunate

One evening, a few weeks after I started reading Rael's books, I decided to try something. Toward the end of the first book, there is an explanation of how one might try to contact the Elohim telepathically. The passage said that telepathic contact was the origin of prayer. It explained that if a person would like to try to telepathically contact the Elohim, they could go outside and gaze at the stars, try to place themselves in harmony with the infinite, and intently think of them. If you were fortunate, you might possibly see a sign.

The Elohim recommended meditating as well. I had begun a daily practice and enjoyed it. I meditated that evening and then went outside. I just stepped a few feet outside of the front door and was looking at the carport, which normally housed my roommate's car, as he was gone to a gig that night. Above the carport were a few small, low lying clouds. In Las Vegas there are so many lights that any low lying clouds look like they are glowing from the inside. Standing there, I tried to place myself in harmony with the infinite by recalling the feeling in my meditation. I then thought intently about the Elohim and my desire to meet them one day. I opened my eyes and was shocked to see a light shining on the roof of the carport. I looked up and saw no helicopter, nor any other object which could have a spotlight. Even if a plane could somehow have a spotlight there would be no way to have such a light remain stationary on the roof of the carport. There was nothing in the sky, but the light was there. When I realized what was happening, I got chills all over and dashed inside.

That was it. I had my proof. I decided to join the Raelian Movement, and I couldn't wait to make it official. The process of joining the RM was simple. The ceremony is very short. An authorized Raelian, known as a Guide (also called a priest), wets their hands with water, places one hand on the person's forehead, and the other at the back of their head. They close their eyes and try to telepathically transmit the unique genetic frequency of the new member to the Elohim, who are in close location on any of the four designated days each year. Since one's genetic code is different than anyone else, this was the way in which a person officially recognizes the Elohim as humanity's creators. The other requirement for adhering to the RM was to sign a document that states you are officially joining. The RM considers itself a religion even in the countries who do not recognize it as such. So if one was baptized into the RM, they would need to sign an act of apostasy to leave one religion and be coherent in joining another. I had, literally, seen the light, so I was ready for whatever the Elohim asked.

Due to my extensive research, I was in the perfect position to speak publicly on the Movement. I gave lectures based on documented materials that proved how carbon and other dating methods were inaccurate, UFOs were in artwork hundreds of years ago, images of ETs were on ancient petroglyphs, and more. I could out-debate anyone willing to accept the facts I presented. But I would eventually learn that the mind loves facts. The heart loves for no reason.

Chapter 9
The Greatest Gig

I continued to work as a professional musician and singer in Vegas, and in 1997, I landed a great full-time gig in a vocal ensemble at the Excalibur hotel. I started by subbing for a friend, but eventually ended up permanently replacing him when he found another gig he liked more. The day's performance ended at 4 p.m., so I also worked at night. Within about a year, I had saved enough to put a down payment on my first home. That gig ended just after 9/11 in 2001. Many people were afraid to travel after the tragedy, so the shows in Las Vegas were heavily affected by it.

In 2003, the Las Vegas housing market was booming. I decided to sell my home so I could buy a bigger one to make more money in appreciation. Right after I bought my bigger home, I found myself without work due to the prolonged effect 9/11 had on the entertainment industry. I had been in Las Vegas for over seventeen years, and until then I had never needed to go out and look for work. One Tuesday, I thought I would start at the south end of the strip and work my way north over the next week. Mandalay Bay was the furthest south, so that's where I decided to go. I walked into the lounge where a band was getting ready to start. I stood over by the sound booth, and one of the guys on the stage started walking toward it. I figured he was going to ask the sound man something. He instead walked up to me and introduced himself as Jimmy.

"You are Ricky, right?" he asked. I nodded. "If you're not working, I would like to hire you. Here's my card. Give me a call tomorrow."

It turned out that I had subbed for his wife's band a couple of years earlier, and she had given me a great reference. He gave me a start date for two weeks out, but I had the RM seminar coming up in four weeks and couldn't miss that. I felt I was working for humanity in the RM. I was dedicated to these seminars, and I had lost gigs before when the band leader did not agree with my beliefs and hired someone else when I went to the seminar. It wasn't a problem for me. That was my priority, and I would be happy to find something else. I always did. I told Jimmy that I needed to go for two weeks not long after he wanted me to start and that I understood if that would be a deal breaker. He said, "No, I still want to hire you." His wife's compliments two years before clinched the gig for me. I didn't even have to audition for the new band. So my very first stop in trying to find work landed what would be over a nine-year gig, and it was the best band I've ever played in. We had a house gig at Margaritaville for well over eight of those years. My luck continued.

Playing in Jimmy's band meant almost no rehearsals. The band was just that good. This also meant I had tons of free time to work more for humanity and write music. What a great life! I had spent thousands of hours writing music since 1995, but I was never a great songwriter. There were two exceptions. One was "Give It All" and the other was "We Are One." (The reason I mention these two is that they would prove to be prophetic in the next eight years as I found *The Law of One* books. My Higher Self was leading me there. It would just take a few more years to get to the heart.)

In January of 2009, the economy was tanking badly, and I knew I would probably be losing the homes I had invested in. This indeed happened the following year. It was around that time that I decided to do something I had been postponing, a yoga class. I knew I would like it, and I sure did. It happened to be a *Bikram* class, meaning it was around 108 °F and about fifty percent humidity. The room was packed, thus the humidity and heat kept rising. I was stuck in the back corner and, of course, learned later that people tried to avoid that corner because it was hotter. About three months later I discovered a *vinyasa* practice that is where one posture is linked to the next through breath. I fell in love with yoga, and it is still a huge part of my life – not just postures but all of yoga. Going to that class was a pivotal event in my life.

On October 11, 2011, I had to make a decision regarding Lillian, my beloved cat. We had been together for seventeen years and had a special connection. I could toss her over my shoulder, and she'd stay as long as I held her. She'd sleep under the covers in the winter and at the foot of my bed in warmer weather. She was only about seven pounds, a grey Tabby. Around two months earlier, she went into hyperthyroidism. Being as small as she was, there was nothing I could do to keep weight on her. She had also started defecating outside of her litter box, meaning that she was in pain. That October day, the vet looked me in the eye, and I knew what she was conveying. I held Lillian close while the vet put her down. As I passed by the front desk to pay, the woman said there is never a fee for this service. (All About Cats in Las Vegas is a wonderful facility.)

I drove home numb. I knew that it was the humane thing to do. Being in my head those years also meant that I knew it was even the logical thing to do. Arriving home, I cleaned up Lillian's last couple of "accidents." Pooter, my other cat who was also a gray Tabby, was under my bed. She had never rested there. She knew that Lillian didn't come home with me. She stayed under the bed all day and all night. The next morning when I woke, it finally hit me. I was no longer numb, but in the deepest emotional pain I had ever experienced. (And it still is, to this day.) Lillian was no longer at the foot of my bed. I fell apart, in tears, several times a day. There was no consolation, though several friends tried. I didn't want to go home from my gig at night. I knew I would be in the same space without her. I couldn't eat. Every time I woke, I would curl into a fetal position and sob.

Up to that point in my life, I rationally believed that people create bonds. Oxytocin and other such hormones cause us to bond with others, creating what I considered a form of addiction, thanks to scientific reports I had read. That was a logical explanation for the pain we feel when faced with losses like this. I tried to discount the pain I was feeling as only hormones. I tried to stick to my rational guns. But the loss I was feeling was so intense that I could have sworn I saw Lillian walk by in the corner of my eye. I walked outside one of those evenings and looked up at the stars. I was silently asking myself and whoever might be listening (I thought the Elohim would hear me.), *What is happening here? I don't believe in a soul. I know this is just hormones. But how is this so powerful?* This was the first time that I started to believe that maybe, just maybe, there is something else going on here. At the very least, I was thinking, *Maybe it's just the energy we exchanged together which is causing me to feel ripped apart now that she's no longer here in this space with me.* It took seven full days and nights for the deepest pains to subside. It would be a few more years, however, until I was ready to understand more.

Chapter 10
The Good Fight Continues

By this time I had many responsibilities within the Movement such as USA National Guide, writing press releases and commentaries. Rael eventually appointed me as head of continental legal affairs. Not long after that, he appointed me North American Continental Guide, which meant I presided over many hundreds of members. Being the head of continental legal matters as well as assisting for the planetary legal department meant there was no shortage of good fights to be had. Sometimes the Movement was defamed, and steps would need to be taken to try to get a retraction from those telling half truths, false accusations, or outright lies. I did this all while continuously trying to bring aid and justice to humanity, championing issues of human rights, religious freedom, the Gay Rights Movement, etc.

Other times the good fight meant taking the fight to someone. The RM had a liberal stance on nudity and sexuality. It wasn't surprising that the Catholic Church disapproved, and they accused the RM of many things, including pedophilia. However, the RM supported sexual freedom only between consenting, legal adults. On the other hand, the Catholic Church itself had real scandals that were beginning to be uncovered. People tend to trust their leaders. Anyone who questions authority are considered conspiracy theorists. For many years, no one could believe that Catholic priests and bishops could be involved in such things. But after so many former victims came forward, the world had no choice but to face the truth. It took decades for people to face it, but pedophilia was a real issue within the Catholic church.

With our attorney, I was successful in filing a lawsuit in the United Kingdom against the former pope, Ratzinger, who had formerly been in charge of handling the increasing number of exposed pedophile cases during the time of Pope John II. Instead of prosecuting the priests who had been abusing children, Ratzinger and his subordinates had helped relocate the priests to keep it quiet. Our attorney and I were surprised that the British government accepted the lawsuit. We figured they would immediately block it. But even if they did, this was good for generating attention to the Movement's defending human rights and shedding more light on what we considered the dark forces within the Vatican. If the case were to have been able to be prosecuted, I am confident that the church would have lost billions. Some diocese even filed for bankruptcy in order to avoid the financial losses. Our lawsuit was filed in 2010 while Ratzinger was visiting the UK. The Vatican, being recognized as a sovereign country, meant that the presiding pope is considered a head of state and cannot be sued. But the former pope is not a head of state. Within a few weeks, however, the right eyes in the British government saw the lawsuit, and it disappeared. I personally believe that means the British government was complicit in those crimes as well.

I remained at my post in the good fight as more years passed. It was about that time that I met a woman with whom I quickly fell in love. Jenny was a dancer in a very long running production show on the Strip. I met her at a yoga studio I frequented where she taught Pilates. She friended me on Facebook, and we started chatting online. The conversation quickly went to human consciousness, and I liked that. We went to dinner, and there was a magical connection. After eating at my favorite Indian restaurant, we went to a small frozen custard stand that had been a local landmark for over fifty years. I raised the tailgate on my Nissan Murano and we sat, chatting. Our chemistry quickly lead us to a lot of laughter. She was originally from the UK and had the British sense of humor (spelled humour to her) I have always enjoyed so much. Within a couple of months she moved in with me, and it was wonderful. We made each other laugh. She was kind and gentle. She was sincere and transparent. While years of meditation had refined my sensitivity, Jenny's presence was softening me more. She would say "golly" instead of four letter words that others would say. She would communicate with a gentle tone and was overall a kind, sensitive, sincere, humble, and funny woman.

During our time together, I started feeling several things shifting within me. I was not working in band situations that were in any way fulfilling, and most of all, I started getting some sort of inner call to move back to Kansas City. It was just this crazy thought that kept surfacing. *You're going back to KC.* The thought would surface several times a day, and I had no idea why. It had been thirty years since I left, and I never wanted to return. Even the thought visiting gave me the willies. But the Voice was haunting me. *KC,* it said.

Jenny and I went to visit Kansas City in December 2013 and had a perfectly delightful time. I realized that if she were with me, I could be there. We even spoke about the possibility of moving there and discussed the idea of finishing the basement of my dad's home and living in it. While before, the idea of KC was sour, Jenny by my side would change everything. I could do KC or anyplace else with her there.

But suddenly, after returning to Las Vegas, Jenny became closed off. I asked her if I had done anything to harm our relationship. She said no, but I could feel that the energy between us had changed. A week or so later, she told me that her ex-boyfriend had texted, wishing her a Merry Christmas, and that she started thinking of him and missing him. I could feel that her heart just wasn't in our relationship, and I have never been one to try to keep someone from doing what they feel they need to do. We parted, and unfortunately for me, she didn't really want to stay in contact. I assumed her decision was because she was back with her ex, and she confirmed that a couple of weeks later. However, I will always be grateful for our time together.

The inner call to go back to Kansas City persisted despite my attempts to ignore it. I went for another visit early September 2014 to look at the town again. I tried like heck to imagine fitting in and possibly retiring there one day. The place still gave me the creeps.

Upon my return to Las Vegas in September, I began my yoga teacher training which would last for ten weeks. It was 200 hours over those weeks, with twice the hours in home study, and that Voice was there the whole time. Something else was going to happen. It was Kansas City and I knew it. I kept asking myself, *Why? I don't like it there. Why am I even thinking about Kansas City? Is it my parents? Will they need me?* My parents were in their upper seventies at that time, and they each lived alone. Being there for them was the only reason I could come up with from my rational mind, also mitigating guilt for possibly abandoning them when they may have needed me. But deeper inside there was an undercurrent of it being something else.

Chapter 11
Relief and Freedom

Though it had been faint, it was sometime in 2012 when I started feeling a sense of incoherence within the RM. Throughout all those years, within the most devoted volunteers in the RM, there was sometimes a friendly competition to see how much time and energy we could contribute. After all, we were trying to help save humanity. There could be no bigger cause in our opinion. I was starting to fatigue, though. Having been among the top four or five leaders on the planet, I began to increasingly notice disagreements among some of the leaders. After I was named Continental Guide, I noticed other bishops questioning my decisions among themselves, then questioning me. That directly went against protocol. Being one who is open for discussion, I tried to invite the dialogue. But if I did not decide to do something the way they had decided among themselves would be better, they would not let up. In other cases, a fellow bishop would try to skirt our guidelines in place when it fit their agenda, but invoke the same rules when they served their own opinions. I observed some leaders, sometimes not so politely, accusing other bishops of "un-Raelian things." Plain and simple, it was politics. I had never liked politics, and I was constantly in the middle of them. Thanks to the Voice starting to whisper in 2012, and thanks to Jenny's softening me over our time together, I became even more sensitive to the politics. I didn't want to leave my post in the good fight, but I started to ask myself, *How can inner politics be anything resembling the good fight?*

These events forced me to face the reality that my responsibilities in the RM were less pleasurable than the many years prior in which I truly felt I was in service to humanity. I was sincerely in service to our Creators, and I had been proud to be where I was. While I felt I would be betraying the Elohim if I were to resign, I also began to feel as if I were trying to tread water while wearing a waterlogged coat. During those years, I had also lost my homes to the market crash. I was actually relieved to have let them go. It felt good to stop fighting to hold on to them. This was another of the battles that was starting to lead me to the thought, *I no longer want to participate in resistance of any kind.*

In November 2014, after my yoga teacher graduation, I finally decided to resign from the RM. Up until that moment, I thought I would feel guilty for abandoning my part in trying to help humanity. However, the very second I pressed the send button on my resignation email, I felt an enormous lightness. I felt like I had shed twenty pounds. Over the next few weeks, I experienced a lot of emotions. I felt like a battered wife who finally had the courage to leave the marriage. My new and well-earned freedom was wonderful, yet I had no idea of the deep healing which was just starting to take place. As this book shows, the healing would take a while. A fellow bishop, Charles, had actually resigned only minutes before I had for the same reasons. I received his resignation email just as I was finishing my own. I mention him here because he worded it well when he said he felt like he was in a boxing match he never wanted to be in.

The moment I resigned, I felt an undercurrent of the decision that I was no longer anti-anything. I would now only speak about what I support instead of what I may be against. Looking back on that now, it is possible that was the beginning of my twelve-inch journey from the head to the heart. Flipping that switch changed my life in indescribable ways, even if it took years to do it. While walking the path toward truth and justice I adhered to as a child, I had finally discovered that even the good fight is still perpetuating separation.

Though I was unaware of it at the time, the reasons I resigned turned out to be the very first two doors into yoga. Over the next couple years, I would discover a practice based on kindness and speaking truthfully. *Ahimsa* means non-harming, or kindness, and *Satya* means speaking and thinking truthfully. I believed I had been kind to people, some of whom I felt were not being so kind. I actually addressed that exact thing in my resignation letter to the RM. My closing statement in my resignation letter was, "One should not mistake politeness for kindness." The RM leaders were very polite. I just didn't find some of them to be kind. That's what politics are to me. Regarding speaking truthfully, I had also discovered that there had been at least one lie carried out at the highest level of the RM. Ever since my toy rifle was stolen in chapter one, I have been on the seeker's path to the truth. I do not personally believe that any good can come from lies or half-truths that claim to be for the greater good.

As my time away from the RM progressed, I started to ask myself questions objectively. *Had I been in a cult? Was it all a lie?* It would be a couple of years before I started piecing together some things I had seen in the RM in a different light. A later chapter will explain this in detail. But at this point, all I knew was that something big, something at my core, on the most fundamental level, was shifting inside of me.

Chapter 12
The Move

Over the two months following my resignation, the nagging Voice became louder and even more frequent. It repeated, *Kansas City,* and I volleyed back with a firm no. It continued to haunt me. After three months of torment, I had no fight whatsoever left in me. So, in February 2015, I called my parents and told them I would be moving back to KC. I still couldn't understand why. I very much resented this nagging Voice for telling me that I was supposed to go back to the place I had wanted to avoid for decades. Most of all, I could not understand why I was being pushed (and it felt like a shove) back to KC. It would eventually be made very clear, but at that point, I was despondent.

I planned to depart on April 5. I find it difficult to put into words the emotions I was feeling over the following eight weeks. My heart was breaking. I loved my life out West. I posted my farewells on Facebook to the Las Vegas community I had known for thirty years. It felt like I needed to do that so as to actually commit to the move. I received far more outreach than I ever expected. I just wanted to send gratitude to all the musicians, agents and friends with whom I played for the previous three decades. Their outpouring of kindness only amplified my emotions. They even threw me a rather large going away party which was so kind, yet deepened the emotions more. It all made my imminent departure even more bitter.

I had hired a mover, and about a week before the planned move date, he asked if it would be alright if he picked up everything a couple of days early since he was working several moves at the same time. Again, at this point I was in no condition to resist absolutely anything, so I agreed. He came on a Thursday, and I was leaving for KC on that Easter Sunday.

I spent the weekend without any furniture. I slept on the floor with my two cats. None of us had any idea what we were in for. With no furniture in the house, they knew something was up, and like me, they liked their life just the way it was. Sunday went as planned. I taught my farewell class in Las Vegas, and it was emotional for all in the room. These were not just friends. They were fellow yogis. *Kula.* My tribe.

Following class, I took a shower and packed my odds and ends in my Murano. I placed my boys in their carriers and put them in the car and drove. Anyone who has cats knows the howl they make when in a car. My heart echoed their sad cries. I let them out of their carriers within five minutes, and they roamed around wondering what in the world was happening. Charly succumbed on the console between the seats. I still have a picture of him from that moment, and it will always invoke the heaviness of that day. Freddy paced in the back, finally surrendering next to the litter box. Within about an hour they had had enough of stressing and simply curled up together on the floor behind the passenger seat. During the rest of the thirty-hour sojourn, they slept for all but a tiny portion.

In the late afternoon, moroseness resurfaced as I looked in the rear view mirror and watched my life of thirty-two years fade away with the desert's elegant sunset. I drove until a little past the halfway point and got a rather seedy motel that would accept cats. We got up around 9 a.m., and I loaded the three of us and the litter box in the car and drove. As I went further east, I saw more of the fundamental Christian influence with billboards reminding everyone about hell and damnation. This was one of the reasons I didn't want to be in the region. As I drove, I also had the heavy feeling that I had somehow failed in my life of thirty plus years, and I still didn't understand why I was returning to Kansas City. Finally reaching the metro area that evening, driving east instead of west on the last stretch of the local freeway as I had done in 1983, I was lost. I had listened to that Voice, but had no idea why I was returning. We arrived at my dad's house at dusk on April 6, 2015.

The mover arrived the next day and put all of my furniture in the basement, which was half finished in that it was divided into two equal halves by some old, tan paneling from the Fifties. The smell of the old basement was much the contrary to my life in the desert for thirty years. I did the best I could to arrange my things into creating an underground living space.

When I do something, I go all in. I went to the DMV the next day. I was putting my new Missouri license plate on (HL1 B3E) when my beloved father, the kindest and most humble man I know innocently commented, "Hey! It almost looks like it says hillbilly!" You might imagine my emotion in that moment. Over the next two months, it rained fifty-six days, and I missed the blue skies of the desert even more.

The following day, I started going to yoga studios. Yoga was the only friend I had there even if I had lost my tribe out west. I hoped that yoga could get me through the shock. I also needed to find studios to teach as I wanted to continue to hone my teaching skills. I visited a new studio every day, and within a couple of weeks someone offered me a class that I gladly accepted. One turned into two, three, and within a few weeks I was teaching about six classes a week. There is a saying that "Midwesterners love their real estate" meaning that things are very spread out there.

Between teaching, looking for other studios to teach, as well as my regular yoga practice, I was soon driving 500 miles a week for the first few months, and my low mileage car went to average pretty quickly.

My family was thrilled at my return. I tried like heck to put on a brave face even if on the inside, I was struggling. Now that I am familiar with the term, I see these years of my life as the poem, "The Dark Night of the Soul," even though I did not believe in a Soul at the time.[7] I was lost in every way possible with the exception of yoga. My heart ached to be back out west. Everywhere I looked in KC only reminded me of my years of just wanting to leave the place. I stayed as busy as I could practicing and teaching yoga. I was trying to create a new life. Trying to keep my mind off the fact that I was back.

What I did really enjoy was cooking for my dad, doing the shopping and doing anything to help that he would let me. I also enjoyed taking mom to lunch and seeing my sisters, even though we didn't get to see each other nearly as often as I was seeing my dad. But in no way, shape or form did it feel like home. Everything I saw reminded me of how much I

---

[7] Tolle, Eckhart. "Eckhart on the Dark Night of the Soul." Eckhart Tolle. https://www.eckharttolle.com/eckhart-on-the-dark-night-of-the-soul/.

had wanted to leave there and every time I was driving west, I wanted to keep driving. Every sunset reminded me of home.

I had an old friend in KC who was a pretty successful musician. He had actually played in Vegas for several years, too. He introduced me to several musicians there, but apparently it just wasn't meant to be. I couldn't find any music work. The thing is, I didn't really miss it. Truthfully, I wasn't even wanting to look for music work. It felt like that chapter of my life was closing. Yoga had, in all of its intrigue, struck a kind of primordial chord deep within me. I was being reacquainted with something from a distant past. This meant that three major changes had taken place in only four months. I was living in KC, and I was teaching yoga for a living instead of music. What I thought to be giant leaps of change would eventually later prove to have been only the entrance ramp to the freeway, as there were way bigger changes on the way. But at the time, I could not have imagined what would happen.

Chapter 13
My Introduction to the Heart

A couple of months after arriving in KC (June 2015), I started feeling some pins-and-needles sensations in my hands and feet. Within a week it spread to my arms and legs. This waxed and waned in no discernible pattern, and it still happens to this day. (It's strongest in my feet, lower legs, hands, and forearms, and it is happening in my hands as I type this.) I had two chiropractors at the time, and we all assumed there was a pinched nerve in my neck. After I finally understood what the cause was, one of them admitted to me later that he didn't think he would be able to help me with the issue. This feeling would eventually spread throughout my body which I will explain, to the degree I am able, later.

Remember the band I joined in 1983 that got me out of KC? It turned out that the drummer, Chad, had a cousin in the KC area. I remembered meeting him and his wife, Rita, in 1983 while we were rehearsing in St. Louis. Chad told me that Rita was a yoga teacher in KC and suggested I call her if I would like to find out more about the KC yoga community. I called Rita, letting her know I would like to find studios where I could teach. She told me what she could about the yoga scene even though she was no longer teaching, since having invested her efforts into energy healing. A few days later, she texted me telling me about a studio owned by a woman named Grace that might be a good fit for my style of yoga. Grace and I met a few days later, and she soon offered me a couple of classes per week. She quickly became my main yoga mentor as well as my best friend there, and my teaching improved quickly under her soft, yet sometimes firm, guidance.

Grace had also been deeply involved in many things regarding energy healing, channeling, working with crystals, sacred geometry, and a long list of things I did not believe in. At her studio, she would regularly host a man by the name of Dr. Rich Fine, who was considered to be skilled in these things.[8] He was known to be able to trance channel a being by the name of Kahotep. I was told that this meant that Rich was able to go into a trance like state, and facilitate communication with a higher dimensional being who could then speak through Rich's mouth. I was skeptical, but I went for the sake of entertainment. At the end of these sessions, one is invited to sit close to him and receive a blessing and/or ask a private question. Of course, I didn't have a question since I didn't believe in any of those things. He made me a little uncomfortable when he volunteered the information, "My dear, let yourself be loved." Being

---

[8] "Meet Dr. Fine." Dr. Rich Fine, SMD, GMT, RMT. http://www.drrichfine.com/meet-dr-fine.

Raelian for those years was all about love, so I had a bit of an internal incredulous reaction even if I remained silent. The evening was interesting, and I enjoyed being in the atmosphere, where I indeed felt a lot of love and harmony. But again, I only saw it as entertainment.

It was still June and building a new life in KC meant, as a yoga teacher, I was going to as many studios as possible trying to find my tribe. I desperately missed my friends out west. Seeing them on Facebook was like salt in a wound that was unable to heal. I was auditioning for a new studio one day and just as a class ended, I happened to glance into the eyes of a gal for about three seconds. All I knew is that she had eyes. I couldn't have told you if she had hair, legs, or anything else. Three seconds of looking at the entire universe in her blue eyes seemed like an hour. She smiled and introduced herself as Karla. She had a certain energy that I had never felt before, and I was drawn to her. We had a short conversation, but in that time, she alluded to the fact that her ex had the kids that weekend. I was hoping that meant she was interested in me. I'll be honest here that I tried to Facebook stalk her, but I could not find her. I was finally able to bump into her about a few weeks later in class. We chatted after class and exchanged numbers. I called her that evening, and it turned out that she had also unsuccessfully stalked me on Facebook. Her birthday was coming up in the following week and I hinted that I was sure she would have a good time on her birthday, and she replied with what I hoped to hear: She had no plans, and her boys would be with their dad. I joked that I promised to never forget her birthday (July 22), asked her to dinner. She immediately said yes.

We decided to meet at a sushi restaurant. It was a hot, humid Sunday afternoon. At about the midpoint for our separate drives, on otherwise seemingly deserted roads and coming from opposite directions, we ended up at the same intersection. We both took it as a good omen. I remember the scene vividly as we were each getting out of our cars. When she stepped down out of her SUV, she was wearing a blueish print sun dress that fanned to the left as her long brown hair followed. It felt like we both knew it would be a fun date. When our food arrived I took my first bite and started nodding my head and saying, "Mmm." She laughed and said she does the exact same thing and that we are a good match. I was overjoyed to hear that because I felt the same thing. As we started spending more time together, I quickly bonded with her young boys, which of course pleased her. I began to think, *Maybe, just maybe, my heart could be in KC as well as out west.*

That same month, I was taking a class at Maya

Yoga, located in one of the oldest parts of downtown KC. Like many cities, the oldest parts were once abandoned but now thriving following renovation. We had just finished practicing, and one of the students introduced me to the teacher, Gwen. During our introduction, the student also told me that Gwen had an interesting story about her brother. Gwen then told me of her brother having been a very mean spirited person for the past 15 or so years, although he had not been so when younger. Gwen said that she asked her brother to meet with a woman by the name of Toby Evans.[9] Toby was supposedly a healer of some sort who could open peoples' Akashic Records (I had no idea what that was.), do a Mid Life Therapy (I didn't believe in that.), Soul Retrieval, (Uh-uh.) Numerology (Nope.), and a whole laundry list of other esoteric skills which, again, I had not believed in.

Gwen is a rather jovial, lighthearted woman, and I felt she was authentic as any real deal yogi is. Gwen said that in that one visit, her brother instantly became kind and generous. She said that Toby had removed a negative entity that was attached to him, and this entity had been causing his mean behavior. My curiosity was finally piqued, and I decided to flirt with that which I did not believe in. I thought I'd go see Toby, even though I didn't pull the trigger on the

[9] Evans, Toby. "Welcome." Sagebrush Exchange. https://www.sagebrushexchange.com/.

visit until two months later, on September 10, 2015.

Toby lived out in the middle of Missouri, surrounded by tall prairie grass in late summer. I saw pickups, cows, and road kill everywhere. These were ominous reminders of my discomfort in the region. When I arrived, she invited me into her comfy studio. It was set up like a guest house/art studio, and several of her artistic creations dressed the walls. The studio had a distinctive Native American vibe. She asked if I was coming to her for anything in particular. Not believing in this stuff, I did not know where to start, so just told her I was curious what she might discover about me. She picked up some divining rods and walked around me. Stopping about six inches behind me, she told me that the back side of my body was almost completely depleted energetically. Skeptical as I was, I didn't say anything. I'm guessing my blank stare said enough, though.

We sat down and she asked me for my birth date and a couple of other things. I summarized my story, that I moved to KC to help my parents, that I did not like it there, and that I had resigned from an organization ten months before. That's all I remember telling her. She added some numbers together according to my date of birth. She said, "You're a thirty-two/five," and explained some of what my numbers meant. I had no verbal response but was thinking, *Okay. Sooo?*

She then said she would open my Akashic Records, and recited a prayer. As she spoke, I started to feel her sincerity. Whether I believed in the woo-woo factor or not, I definitely felt her authenticity. After a few seconds she said, "Your records are open...I don't know if you feel anything but..." I interrupted her to say that I felt a huge wave of love, and she replied, "That's exactly what it is." It was so powerful that I started crying but pulled back the tears because I wasn't sure if I really felt anything or if I was just convincing myself I was.

Upon opening my Akashic Records and continuing to "work my numbers" as she called it, she started telling me things about myself that no one but me could possibly know. I was not ready to be impressed, but I listened. She spent a good 30 minutes telling me about my numbers. According to her, she was using some sort of numerological system that she believed gave her information regarding the lessons and experiences my Soul wanted to experience in this particular lifetime. Some things she told me resonated, but I just wasn't ready for all of it at the time. In hindsight, I see the twelve-inch journey had not actually begun, but I was starting to pack my bags.

While claiming to be in my Akashic Records

she said, "You came here for your parents as you think you did. But your parents were just the bait on the hook to get you here. You really came here to work through some karma." I suddenly had a pit in my stomach. In that moment I was thinking, *What in the hell did I do because I don't want to be here!* but I said nothing. I was squirming inside. I felt like I was being punished for something. Pondering her remark, I had an inner passive/aggressive reaction. I was thinking things along the line of, *I am a good person,* as well as simultaneously feeling guilt for something bad I had done, not even knowing what that thing was. I quickly went deeper into my rational mind in order to dismiss the idea that I was supposed to be cleaning up karma. I did not believe in all that from my time in the RM. We didn't believe in things like **Souls**, channeling, Akashic Records, and I had only resigned ten months earlier. It was still too early for the twelve-inch journey to start.

As Toby went on, she gained my attention. If for no other reason, I could truly feel that she was sincere. Referring to the Akashic Records she said, "Your masters, teachers and loved ones are telling me that your resignation from that organization [the RM] was your graduation". I could not have agreed more with her more as this is exactly how it felt. She said, "They were with you when you did that," meaning my masters, teachers and loved ones were there supporting me. Upon hearing this, I felt that wave of love again and again, and I began crying.

I could not explain it at the time, but I now see that as my heart was starting to call deeper to my head. The twelve-inch journey was starting. Where Jenny had softened me with her gentle spirit, Toby was skillfully exposing me to the different vehicles I would need for the varied terrains along the journey.

Toby then did some more testing on me. One in particular she did was sway testing, or tilt testing. Sway testing is a type of kinesiology, when the body responds to questions without letting the mind get in the way of the answers. Though I didn't understand it at the time, the technique is based on the idea that one's unconscious mind is always connected to Spirit, where all information is available. Then the unconscious mind has access to answers the conscious mind does not. When one stands still and asks a question, they will tilt forward if the answer is yes. If it's a no, they tilt back. She asked a question, and I repeated it in order to get a yes or no answer. By asking a series of yes or no questions, she was honing in on detailed information. It was working, and I was so surprised that I laughed a couple of times. She asked many things, such as if I had any negative entities attached to me. I tested no to that question. She then asked if I had any other beings attached to me. We got a yes. She asked if it was a male. I tilted back, meaning it was a female. She asked if the woman had died peacefully. She had not. Toby then asked if she was murdered. No. "Had she died in an accident?" Yes. "Was it a car crash?" Yes. Continuing with a series of questions, this entity told us that she had been a young woman who had died in a car accident due to the driver having been under the influence of alcohol as well as other things. Toby asked if the being had been attached to me for more than a year. Yes. "More than ten years?" Yes. "More than twenty?" Yes. Eventually, Toby narrowed it down to more than thirty years when this woman had attached to me, during my era of heavy drug use.

Toby said that when some people die, they can remain earthbound because they're not aware that they have actually died. If they had certain addictions themselves, they often like to attach to someone who also has similar addictions in order to stay connected to those types of feelings. Toby proceeded in questioning the entity, and I was tilting forward and backward like I had been doing this my whole life. Invoking archangel Michael for protection for this female entity, she persuaded her to leave my body and go to where she could be back with her own Higher Self in higher realms of some sort.

The next question she asked was if there were any other attachments to me, and we got a yes.

Following a line of questioning, Toby discovered that the Atlantean priestess Isis and I had a connection, and that we had apparently been up to some things which were less than advisable at the time. Toby asked if anyone died due to our mischief. I immediately started wondering about that karma I was supposed to clean up. Though I was not yet convinced any of Toby's witchy woman stuff was real, I was still happy to get a no to that question. When questioning why Isis was attached to me, Toby was able to narrow down that Isis had vowed to always protect me, as I had once been protecting her. Toby asked Isis if she would like to go back. I honestly don't remember these precise details of that moment, but I do remember Toby asking me if I wanted to say anything to Isis before she left. I started crying (like I am now remembering this moment) and thanking Isis for her loyalty. I was sobbing profoundly while feeling an enormous amount of love going through me.

The next thing Toby asked me was if there were any false light beings attached to me, and we got a resounding yes. She asked, "Are there more than five?" Yes. "Are there more than ten?" Yes. "Twenty?" Yes. "Fifty?" Yes. She worked her way up to ninety and said she hadn't seen that many before. She asked Archangel Michael to place a protective cloak around these beings so that they could go where they needed to go. The cloak was apparently needed so that their "superiors" would not notice these minions are leaving their post, being me.

Before I left, she checked my aura which had been so depleted around my back. At the beginning of the session, she was standing only six inches behind me, indicating a very weak field. By the end, she was standing twenty feet behind me against the door. She said she could keep going, and she was confident that it would go out much further if she were to open the door and walk out. She asked if my lower back was a weak spot for me. It definitely was, and it turned out that the car crash entity had been attached to my lower back. I had also injured my back in a motorcycle accident. Toby said these beings usually attach to one's weakest point, and this was definitely the case for me.

She then had me walk her labyrinth in the twelve-foot tall prairie grasses. I clearly remember my state of mind in those thirty or so minutes asking myself, *Do I really believe any of this stuff?* There was just no way for me to process what happened in those three hours. But I knew that I liked Toby. There was a connection of some sort. Over the next few days, the entire experience just sort of faded from my memory. I now understand that was the next step in my twelve-inch journey. At the time, however, I was still resisting. My head liked being in charge.

Chapter 14
Woo-Woo 102

The months passed, and the dreaded KC winter was approaching. I grew accustomed to the pins-and-needles and had given up on finding the solution. Karla and her two young boys had helped me to start believing that I might have an enjoyable life in the Midwest. In December, however, Karla told me that she wanted to have another baby. Treading the waters as I was at the time, I couldn't be the guy for her. We parted company, leaving me grateful for her grounding energy.

By January 2016, the Toby story was four months old, and I had all but forgotten about it. My yoga mentor, Grace, as well as a mutual friend, Nina, had given me a Christmas gift inviting me to do an energy work session for free. It lasted around two hours with me lying on a yoga mat by the alter in the studio. (Yoga studios who endeavor to honor the true spirituality of yoga have small alters that honor certain teachers, mystics, gods, gurus, Jesus, etc.) Grace placed different crystals on my forehead, chest, and all the way down to my waist. She was supposedly mending/healing parts of my energy body, which was still just a lot of meta-talk for me at the time. While she worked, her hands looked like she was holding a needle and thread. It looked like she was sewing or mending. Our other friend, Nina, was sitting to our side on the floor around five feet to my right. She had her eyes closed. Grace told me that Nina was channeling her spirit guides. The alleged guides would see inside my body and then Nina would tell Grace something like, "Silver thread for the throat chakra." I was definitely in another situation where I had no idea what was going on, reminding me of my September visit with Toby.

Grace knew that I did not particularly want to be living in KC at the time (especially in January) and unsolicited by me, she asked Nina, "Can Ricky leave KC yet?" Nina paused and then softly replied, but I couldn't hear what she said. I asked Grace, and she said, "You're home." When I heard that, I had an emotional gut reaction, as well as that initial belly pump one has when they are about to cry. I'm sure you know the feeling. But I did not cry since I had already experienced those emotions countless times regarding moving back to KC. I had learned to navigate all that. Grace and Nina kept working as a team, and about fifteen seconds later, Grace looked at Nina and asked, "What's wrong?" Eyes still closed, Nina was crying. Nina said, "If you won't cry, we will cry for you." That got my attention. Her guides knew exactly what I was feeling. I was still looking like a deer in the headlights but thought, *I am starting to think that all this may be real.*

About twenty minutes later, out of nowhere, Nina said, "He was one of Yeshua's Disciples." (Yeshua was Jesus' real name.) Grace, in her very quiet but confident voice declared, "That is why you are here. All of His disciples, followers, students of the Ancient Mystery Schools, etc. have been called to this region for some reason. I am not sure what that reason is but you're all drawn here. The area is known as the Heart of the Dove." Over time, I would learn that the region in which Kansas City lies is considered the Heart of the Dove in *The Keys of Enoch,* which is a highly revered mystical, esoteric book about the prophet Enoch from the Old Testament.[10] (Enoch was one of only two people who did not die on earth but was taken away by God.)

At the end of that session, with her eyes still closed, Nina told me, "There is a huge and powerful light coming down on you. Whenever you need to feel love, just hold your hands out like this." She was resting the backs of her hands on her thighs, and her palms were facing up. After two hours in the session I left, again, trying to take it all in. Later that day, I tried placing my hands on my thighs as Nina suggested. I felt so much love that I started to cry. After a few days, though, the visit sort of faded from being anything all

---

[10] "Keys of Enoch North America Site." The Keys of Enoch. https://keysofenoch.org.

that important. Yet unbeknownst to me at the time, I had ventured another inch of the twelve.

That same month, I finally accepted that I was indeed now home and had the deep call to renovate my dad's basement in order to make it more homey. It was winter in KC, which typically consisted of gray skies, and I didn't want to spend time in a gray basement. I needed light and color, like out west. I went to work immediately on the 675 square foot space. The primary colors were bright yet earthy yellow, red, and green for the accent wall. I was back to creating, even if it wasn't music, and it felt good. I ordered some curtains and hung those a few days later. It turned out to be the best zen space anyone could hope for.

Over the next three months, I grew to love my life there. It had turned out to be a very mild winter after all, and the fearless colors of spring were brilliant. It no longer bothered me that the trees blocked the sunsets, and I grew to be grateful for how grounding the geographic area is. I had become accustomed to my new life. I still missed my friends in Las Vegas, but seeing them on Facebook gave me a smile instead of an aching heart.

Somewhere along the way, I had traveled yet another inch on my journey. I finally realized that it was not Kansas City I was not comfortable with decades earlier. It was me in my life back in the Eighties. By the time March came around, I had no desire of leaving whatsoever. The lawn mowers were always running somewhere in the neighborhood, and the smell of cut grass reminded me of my childhood in a good way. The lightening bugs and the sounds of crickets and frogs were reminding me that I was living closer to nature, and that felt nice. I was even occasionally playing in a band on top of teaching seventeen yoga classes a week, and I was loving it. I felt like I was home.

Section Two

Chapter 15
And Then It Happened

On May 30, 2016, I was picking up something from a table in the living space I had created, and out of nowhere that same Voice told me clearly, *It's complete. You can leave soon.* Completely stunned, I thought, *Did I really hear that? Are you sure?* In my previous experience with the Voice, it was a gentle nudge, a haunting whisper. There was nothing subtle about the Voice this time. It was a hundred times louder than before. So loud that I actually heard it in my left ear, as if the Voice were just above me and to my left. (At the time, I didn't know if it was a spirit guide or something else. I now believe it was my Soul or Higher Self.) Responding to my question, it said, *Be assured. If it's not complete now, it will be very soon.* The following day I told my dad. The day after, I told my mom. I would probably be going back out west in about four or five months, as the Voice was also telling me that there was something else needing to take place there. But I was in no hurry since I now loved my new home.

Three weeks later, the day before my birthday in June, I was in the general neighborhood of Grace's studio. I knew that Rich would be channeling Kahotep that evening. I had not been to these sessions in seven months, so I thought I would go. I had a strong urge to go without knowing why, but after what I had been experiencing I was starting to know when the Voice was urging me to do something. (I now call it my wife and just do what it tells me to do.) At the end of these channeling sessions, one is invited to sit one-on-one with Kahotep and ask a question and/or receive a blessing. As I started to sit in front of Kahotep, he said, "You have a question." He did not ask me. He told me that I had a question. I did not have a question in mind when I walked up, but what popped out of my mouth was only,"I moved here..." He interrupted me. I was going to ask, "I moved here over a year ago in order to complete something. Is it complete yet?" I didn't say the word karma, but that was what I was thinking of, the karma Toby had originally mentioned nine months earlier. I had only begun to whisper my question when he interrupted me and said, "Not yet but it will be very soon" He told me exactly what Voice had told me three weeks earlier. I was ecstatic. And it wasn't because I could leave KC. As I said, I loved my life there at that point. But I was ecstatic to confirm that the Woo-Woo was real. Even moreso, that the Voice was real and that I was indeed in contact with it. At that moment, I was instantly three more inches closer to the destination of the heart. I understood that I had indeed been on an expedition toward Spirit all along.

Kahotep then asked if I would like a blessing. I said, "Yes, please." But I was thinking, *I would love a blessing, but you won't be able to top what you just said!* I was sitting about two feet in front of Rich and facing his right side. Both of Rich's hands were around the area of my heart and solar plexus area, one in front and one behind. He whispered in an incomprehensible language, and then I felt an energy going through my solar plexus as well as a little higher. It was kind of like a string was being pulled from front to back through my solar plexus. I was almost giddy since all this stuff was becoming so real, and that I could even feel that "string thing" in my solar plexus. When he finished, I thanked him and started to stand. As I started to stand, he placed his hands on my thighs meaning I should sit back down. He said, "My dear, very soon you will be connected with Divine Grace." I was not (and am still not) exactly sure what that is, but I know it's a good thing.

What felt most wonderful is that I then knew I had completed something beyond big on a spiritual level in going to KC. I inherently felt that I succeeded in something that was now liberating me. I started to suspect that the **Voice** was my Higher Self. Freedom has always been extremely important to me, and it was happening. The most difficult things I ever did in

leaving the RM and leaving Las Vegas had now
become the most beautiful thing that ever happened to
me, thanks to the Voice.

Chapter 16
Let the Buzzing Begin

While driving home that evening, I was in awe of what had just happened. It kept going through my head, *It's all real! It's all real!* I was driving the stretch of freeway, which I mentioned saddened me upon my return to KC, but this time it was a triumphant, beautiful homecoming. About ten minutes into the drive that night, the Voice told me to get back to my regular meditation practice. I certainly knew by then – listen.

In my zen space the next day, I lit some frankincense. I had read this was good for calling in angels and the like. I meditated for about thirty minutes. I repeated the following day. It was at that time the next couple of inches were traversed on my twelve-inch spiritual safari. Within one minute of that meditation, my third eye chakra started to buzz or tingle. Immediately after, my crown chakra started doing the same thing. It also felt like someone or something was lightly pressing on my third eye area as well as the crown of my head. Within a few seconds, that combined with what felt like an energy of some sort flowing down from the very top of my crown. For those familiar with electricity, it felt, but in quite a pleasant way, like a few volts were flowing through my head. Then the energy flowed down to my throat chakra. Then the heart. It even went a bit into my solar plexus area, feeling similar to when Kahotep was blessing me two days earlier. It was like a sort of tightness – almost like a feeling of static electricity on my skin, from my solar plexus all the way to the crown of my head. I needed to leave to go teach a yoga class, and the feeling continued as I was driving. I could hardly believe what I was experiencing. Ever since that day, it happens every waking hour of my day, and yes, it's happening right now. It's always happening, and while it can be a little distracting sometimes, if I simply sit and be present in it for a few seconds, it becomes so blissful that tears start to flow.

My conversion to the mystical and esoteric was now complete. In a couple of days, I called Toby in hopes that she would be able to tell me more about what I had experienced with the energy I was feeling in my upper chakras. She said, "Ricky I'm thrilled for you. What you're feeling is that you are tapping into the fifth dimension, and you will be able to do that from now on wherever you go." As I write this, I am still trying to wrap my head around that. All I can say is that it truly feels like I am connected to something not of the same world in which I used to live only three years ago. This energy subsides when I go to bed, but if I focus on it while still awake in bed, it returns immediately.

Over the next few months, I had many other clear confirmations who were telling me, often without my even asking them, the information that Voice had so emphatically told me in May. *It's complete. You can leave...very soon.* It got to the point where I would just laugh out loud. For example, I was at a well known New Age book store in KC looking at some incense. Through my peripheral vision, I saw a woman walk by behind me. Doubling back, she came up to me and said, "Wow! You have so much good energy flowing through you!" This was the first time someone in public called me out on it, and I raised my eyebrows, nodded, and told her that a bunch of things happened to me over the past few weeks and that it felt wonderful, even if I had no idea what it meant. She assured me, "You have a lot of very good things coming your way!"

Another powerful confirmation took place about three months after Kahotep told me it would be very soon. I sat briefly with an acquaintance, Kim, who is a yoga teacher and a channel. She does not trance channel like Rich does with Kahotep. Her type of channeling is when one taps into certain energies from the universe and can then ascertain certain information. (For anyone familiar with the Akashic Records, it seems to be very similar to this.) Up to that point in KC, I had only spoken briefly with Kim two or three times, so she knew nothing about me other than I taught yoga and I had moved to KC from Las Vegas. I sat with her for a short ten-minute session before I was to teach my evening class. She asked me if I had any questions. Still being new to these types of things, I couldn't really think of anything. She said I could ask about health issues or other things. "Sure let's go with that," I said, "What do you see with my health?" She told me that everything looked good but to be mindful of my right foot. I had Plantar fasciitis at the time, and apparently she saw that. Her voice turned to a more enthusiastic tone, and she said, "Your heart chakra is very open." I smiled and told her that was exactly what it felt like. I had not told her anything at all about the energies I was feeling ever since that memorable meditation, but she had obviously seen it. There were no more headwinds in my journey toward the heart.

Then a question popped into mind regarding the karma which Toby mentioned about eleven months earlier. I asked, "Can you tell me, is the karma I was supposed to work through....is it complete yet?" She immediately responded, "It's just wrapping up right now."

By then, I had learned that Spirit (from channeling, Akashic Records, etc.) would not give any information that might interfere with my own path of free will, but I thought I'd push my luck. I asked, "Can you tell what exactly was the karma that I was needing to complete?" She paused and said, "You needed to be in this geographic region. Something to do with an energy exchange that needed to take place in this region." I smiled since it aligned perfectly with what Nina had said about me being a disciple of Yeshua and Grace telling me that it was why I was drawn back to the Heart of the Dove region. I had not told Kim anything at all of my plan to move back out to Las Vegas, yet she went on to say, "You are free to leave and go anywhere you are happy. You have completed what you needed to do here. You are free to go wherever you like now." Like I said, I am all about being free, and I was thrilled to hear this.

Since Kim was so spot on with everything she said, I decided to ask her something about Rael. I would like to state here that I had never once discussed Rael or the RM with her before. I asked her, "Is the man I know as Rael in contact with extraterrestrials?" She paused and replied, "He is in mental contact with them, but not physical. You were right to leave. You had nothing more to learn from him." Once again, without knowing anything about my past, she was accurate regarding my leaving the RM. Based on what she said, I have since begun to get the feeling that Rael is in mental contact with a group of ETs calling themselves Elohim, but the devil is in the details. (Spoiler alert: Remember the more than ninety false light beings Toby found attached to me.) That ten minutes with Kim further sealed-the-deal of all things I never believed in while in the RM.

Before leaving KC, I went to two more sessions with Kahotep. It was then four months after he told me, "Not yet, but it will be very soon," and I only had about four weeks before the planned move. (At the time of this writing, I have now learned that when a non-physical being tells you something will be happening soon, that can mean as little as a week or it can mean decades or more, since they are not a part of living in linear time as you and I are.) I asked Kahotep, "Can you tell me what I'm feeling in my top five chakras and throughout my body?" I was referring to the chakra energies as well as the pins and needles sensations. He once again interrupted me and replied, "Does it not feel good?" in an almost sarcastic tone. (Kahotep sometimes has a sense of humor.) I said, "It feels wonderful! Is it..." Again, he interrupted me saying, "It is preparing you for Divine Grace," which he had told me those four months earlier would be happening "very soon." I asked what was happening, what the tingling was in my chakras, and he said, "Your vibration is being adjusted."

By that time, I had trained with a couple of people and received my certification in opening the Akashic Records as well as another certification in channeling from the same person who trained Kim. I started practicing those things as well as studying many other related esoteric things. Several friends knew I had been doing these trainings and asked if I would channel for them. I became a little nervous. *Will I really be able to do this? I didn't even think this was possible three months ago,* I thought. Two friends, Mike and Amy, were among the people who had asked me to channel for them. They were both yoga teachers at the main yoga studio I taught. I did Mike first. I knew he had recently gone through a divorce but little else. The information came in. *You were right to let her go even if it didn't feel good. Anyway, you have three times the relationship coming your way right now. You've never experienced the amount of love you are about to. I am also getting that you would benefit by going deeper into yoga philosophy at this time in your life.* My rational mind questioned that, but I sent him what I got, and I trusted.

I did Amy two days later. When I got her information, I was doubting myself. It was almost exactly the same as Mike's. *Your next relationship will be the deepest one you've ever had. It will be like nothing else you've experienced. Something else I am getting is that you may want to trust yourself more. This one will be beautiful.* Three weeks later, Amy announced that she was pregnant. Mike was the father. I had not been aware that they were seeing each other, but the information that came in for both of them was correct. They are still happy together as of this day.

I moved back to Las Vegas on October 17, 2016. When the Voice came in around May 30 telling me, *It's complete. You can leave,* I had the hint that October would be the time I would move. The studio I just referred to was redoing their schedule on October 18, so I took that as a sign. Still having my parents' work ethic, I didn't want to leave them short-handed. You will see later that this was no accident, either.

Chapter 17
Vegas Bound – Again

Leaving Vegas eighteen months earlier had been the toughest thing I had ever done, and I was surprised that leaving KC was the second hardest thing I was now doing. I cannot overstate the depth of my emotions: Victorious. Humbled. Amazed. Wondrous. In awe. Gratitude. So much gratitude. And the bliss of the energy flowing through my upper chakras as well as the "adjustment" being done on my body was amplifying all of it.

Throughout the first fifteen months back in Las Vegas, I taught a few classes along with doing a little music work. Mostly, however, I studied all the things I had been exposed to. I read approximately 20,000 pages and viewed hundreds of lectures and interviews on psychics, channeling, Archangels, spirit guides, tarot cards, and anything that I had not believed in for those almost twenty-three years. Woo-woo had become real only two years earlier, and I was trying to make up for what felt like lost time. Once the first couple of inches from the head to the heart had begun in KC, I started to feel like I was late for an appointment of some sort. I wanted more. I was in full research mode, doing what Toby had called "remembering."

I still didn't know how all the meta-pieces fit together, but I had learned to trust my gut. Kahotep, Toby, Nina, and others had opened my eyes. But it would not have been possible had I not listened to the Voice. I was learning to listen and trust that intuition. What else I might discover? All indicators, however, pointed to one source of information. You might simply call it Spirit, Source, or God. I personally do not believe there can be a word for something so unknowable, but you can define it as you will.

Two months after I moved back to Vegas, a musician friend of thirty years passed. We called him Sweet Eddie D. Dozens of musicians were there to pay tribute to Eddie. He had a sense of humor that bounced between innocent and cheeky. More than that, he had an open heart. Eddie would give anything he had to anyone who needed it. In my life as an atheist for over twenty years, I had not been one to attend funerals. I had attended the funeral of another beloved musician friend three years earlier, but it was more out of a sense of social musician obligation. (I miss you Mark, and I see things differently now.) In Eddie's case, however, I felt a call to attend. I had also recently made instant friends with Maria, the wife of a musician friend, Jamie. I became close to both of them after my conversion to the metaphysical. Maria was attending the funeral, but Jamie was at a gig across the country. With a glance across the room, Maria and I knew that we felt more comfortable sitting together at Eddie's more traditional funeral service. We instinctively headed to a pew toward the back of the parlor. As Eddie's son of about twenty-five was honoring his father, I started to see a gold/yellow cloud of some kind hugging the ceiling above Eddie's casket. I squinted a few times to get a better view, but it was there every time I opened my eyes. It slowly moved right, over Eddie's son. Then it went left, over the open casket. It moved right again, staying over Eddie's son. I assumed what I was seeing to be caused by the soft lighting in the room, bringing on eye fatigue.

About three weeks later, I was having lunch with Maria and Jaime. Eddie's name came up, and Maria sassed to the group, "You know, I saw him at the funeral." I flinched to her on my right and bounced back, "You mean that yellow cloud? I saw..." She interrupted, "Yes! You saw it too!" We had both seen Eddie's soul (call it what you like) moving from above his open casket over to above his son.

Over the next six months, I continued to read, view, and study all things "meta" I had recently started to remember. About that time, I went to see a psychic by the name of Kim. I had found her on a local website for the Psychic Eye metaphysical bookstores, who also offer in-house tarot readers, mediums, psychics, etc. I was starting to increasingly trust my intuition, and I felt a connection with her when watching her one-minute promo video on the Psychic Eye web page. When I walked in for our session, she instantly barked, "You're more psychic than me! What are you doing here?" We had a little chuckle over her remark but if I'm honest, I was feeling a little like, *Yeah, I kind of know I am psychic but I'm still new to this. I'm too much in my head and self-doubt to really own all that yet.* I told her just a little of my awakening process over the preceding two years.

Kim said she could see three of my guides there in the room with me. I asked if any of them had a name. She told me she wasn't picking up on any. (That's not unusual since these beings are simply energies, and they only use names in order to help us grasp their existence more clearly.) She said one of my guides was simply a huge, extremely bright column of white light. Kim then said, "August...what's coming in for you in August is huge." She kept repeating, "Wow, it's like you're going to win two lotteries of some sort in August." I understood that she was not referring to money. Incidentally, I had gone to a Tarot reader the previous week who also told me something big was "coming in" for me in August.

By then, Toby was my closest friend. I gave her a call the day after seeing Kim. She started telling me about the upcoming eclipse (August 21, 2017) and that she was "told" to host an event in which around twenty-four people would need to participate in. There would be a couple of types of ceremonies. The purpose would be to bring in the energies from the eclipse, amplify these using quartz crystals as well as pure intent, and then send those energies out to the entire planet. These energies would be helping the planet to heal as well as ascend into higher vibrations (more peaceful, forgiving, and compassionate). Coincidence or not, the eclipse's path of totality would be passing right over Toby's property I had visited in September 2015.

I was thinking, *I wish I knew enough about all this to be able to go there and help.* But I remained shy as, once again, I was still awkwardly navigating my way through all this stuff, even if I had been voraciously reading and doing several forms of energy training for the previous fifteen months. She came to a point in her explanation where she paused and said, "I'm just saying...in case you wanna come." I almost jumped out of my seat and asked her if she really thought I could be a healthy addition to the group. After all, she's been the witchy woman for thirty-plus years and runs in pretty advanced circles. She said, "Are you kidding? All the meditation and study you do? You're likely better than all of us!" Knowing her kind intent, I had no misgivings at all but was only humbled to have received the invitation. I assured her I

101

would be there, and it was an absolutely beautiful and very powerful experience. There were about twelve people in her labyrinth performing a ceremony. I was with Toby and around eight others, doing another ceremony, walking through her nine-pointed crystal vesica garden. This was composed of a couple of hundred quartz crystals of approximately six to eight inches. (Quartz crystals amplify energies.) During the ceremony, the buzzing in my body was off the usual scale of eight to a strong ten. I am always in a state of awe and bliss when being present with this energy, and it was more intense (in a good way) than ever. This energy is not like I "have" more energy for daily activities. For those who have ever placed your tongue on a nine volt battery, the energy feels like a lesser version of that, only not on the tongue. It's like a small amount of electricity, entering at the top of my head (crown chakra) and flowing downward. I didn't connect the dots until weeks later, but that amplified eclipse energy was the "lottery" I would be experiencing. The months passed, and I continued my studies.

In March 2018, the call came in, and the Voice whispered that I would be going back to KC. My left brain asked the Voice if it was sure that I had completed what I was called back to Las Vegas to do. In September 2016 while still in KC, Kim told me that I would be creating something upon my return to the desert. I wanted to be sure I had completed that, whatever it was. I no longer needed to know what it was. Just knowing it was complete was enough for me. I had also been told by the person in KC under whom I trained in channeling, that I would be sitting with a group of people who would see me as a leader of sorts. I assumed this meant me being a yoga teacher, but he said it was something different. Then I remembered the many meditation workshops I had been teaching while being back in Las Vegas. These were extremely popular and often reached maximum capacity.

The Voice then assured me it was complete. I was reminded that I had created, with the mutual coordination of some amazing people that are dear to my heart, a private meditation group where we could share any and all things most people consider fringe or just too "out there." This group was a safe haven for all who felt energies and their own Voices but were not able to share with others who would just wouldn't get it. The bulk of the book you are now reading was complete by that time, and the Voice also reminded me that it had guided me to write it. It told me that I had completed everything I had returned to create.

Then it hit me. I had created a new me. Had I stayed in KC teaching seventeen classes a week and gigging part time, I would have not immersed myself nearly as intensely into my studies. My time back in

Las Vegas provided me with three to eight hours a day for this, and I threw myself head first into all of it. Having not believed in these things while in the RM for twenty-three years, I had the desire to make up for lost time. And it worked. Thanks to the Voice, the path to the heart was becoming more familiar.

The next month, April 2018, I was on an eight-day gig in San Francisco, which was the mother of all gigs in my career. We were playing only three days and had four days off in the middle of the week. The first day off, I decided to head up to Muir woods about sixty minutes away to visit the Redwoods. I had read in the book *The Law of One* that trees can emit enormous amounts of love. I was very sure that I needed to be with these gentle giants. I was not disappointed. I took my shoes off and slowly walked the soft pine trails in complete bliss. It was one of the most religious experiences of my life. This forest was a temple. It exuded a spirituality that was unmistakable. When other visitors would talk to one another, it would shatter the silent symphony and I must admit, I wanted to be there alone. This sacred place emitted a love that was tangible, and for the first time, I began to truly feel on a deeper level the spirituality which indigenous peoples all over the world hold for all things living. These extremely loving beings, so casually called trees, were ancient and sentient. I marveled, sensing how their enormous roots were all communicating within their population.

The next day in my hotel room I received a firm message from the Voice telling me, *You need to be back in KC by June 1.* My first thought was, *Hey, wait a minute. Don't rush me. That's only five weeks away.* My rational mind questioned the caller as usual. I wasn't sure I wanted to run back to KC that soon, but I got the firm reply, *June 1.* The next day, the message was repeated. By then, I trusted the Voice, so I gave thirty-two days notice to the management company for the house I had been renting. I pulled the trigger on the move in a heartbeat and planned the drive for May 30, feeling sorry for my beloved cats having to undergo yet a third drive of 1550 miles.

I returned to Vegas from San Francisco three days later, and I emailed the general manager of Power Life, the main yoga studio I had been teaching at in Kansas City. As I mentioned earlier, I had left on extremely good terms, having planned my move around what would be most convenient for them. I informed her that I would be back June 1. I knew they had opened a third location while I was in San Francisco. I logically assumed that while they might be able to offer me a couple of classes, I would need to wait for more classes to become available. Her reply was a clear conformation of the June 1 message I received.

"The timing couldn't be better. Our new schedule goes into effect on June 4. How many classes would you like?"

I couldn't understand how she could have so many classes open until a couple of days later when they made the announcement that they had been secretly taking over another studio. So I arrived in KC on June 1 and started teaching twelve to fifteen classes a week only three days later. June 1 was indeed the date to be there. I silently winked at the Voice.

Section Three

As I immersed myself in all of the things I had not believed in for over two decades, I began to understand more. I was introduced to many of those things in KC, but I dove in head-first into the deep end of the world of Woo-Woo. I grew to understand meta-talk, and I was, as Toby told me in 2016, remembering. I was remembering what is our birthright and remembering how to discern between the head wanting to know and the heart which has always known. In three years, I had certifications in channeling, opening the Akashic Records, several types of energy healing, and more. Channeling, reincarnation, past lives, karma, Soul contracts, and many other things were constantly in my thoughts thanks to the twelve-inch journey to the heart.

While the first two sections of this book explained what happened to me when awakening to the spiritual and esoteric, this section will explain more of why I believe it took place. So how and why do I believe my twelve-inch journey unfolded? I believe now that my Soul, or Higher Self (define that as you like), was leading me home. The home to where all truth resides is Spirit, the heart. If, as we go on, some things seem unbelievable, don't feel alone. As you have read, I didn't believe in many things until they showed up in such a way that I couldn't deny them. Once I reached that point, I continued digging.

Chapter 18
Terms to Remember

In order to go further into what I discovered, this chapter will go deeper into some of the concepts that were revealed to me in Section Two. I am placing these in the order I believe helps lead into the remainder of this book. I use the word "Soul" throughout this chapter. There are some semantics with this word. Most sources I have studied over these recent years say that our Higher Self is like our "Oversoul." It exists within sixth-density (which we will get into). Our Soul, however, is a smaller portion of the Higher Self, and our Soul is kind of our personality that we carry from lifetime to lifetime. But for the sake of semantics, we will just call it our Soul in this chapter.

Reincarnation and Past Lives

Though defined in a fairly consistent manner, reincarnation is received (or dismissed) somewhat differently all over the world. If it's somehow even possible you are not familiar with reincarnation, it is the idea that a person has multiple lives. Multiple physical lives, that is. We live many lives in order to gain experience and work through karma.

Western religion has not been fond of the idea of reincarnation, though many of its contemporary members are open to the idea. There is even good evidence that Jesus spoke about reincarnation but that the early church removed anything having to do with it. It seems that the leaders wanted people to believe that we only have one chance to "get it right." If we knew we had many lives to learn what was necessary, then we wouldn't try as hard as we would believing we only got one chance. Buddhism, Hinduism, Jainism, and Sikhism are the larger believers in reincarnation. Furthermore, yoga and Gnostic Christianity also assume it to be quite real.

In 1945, the Nag Hammadi scrolls were unearthed in upper Egypt and included additional gospels which had purposely been omitted from the Bible. Respected researcher/author William Henry pointed out that the Gnostic texts actually came from the disciples of Jesus and that they received these teachings from Jesus after he resurrected.[11] Henry says that the texts were largely Jesus' teachings of how to navigate in the afterlife and avoid reincarnating. The Gnostic scriptures were offering people, through knowledge of the self, the way to avoid reincarnating and, instead, remain in a vastly more spiritual realm.

Contemporary science is split in its acceptance of reincarnation. However, there are a growing number of doctors and those in medicine who fully accept it. Dr. Michael Newton[12] and Dr. Ian Stevenson[13] were both hard sells when it came to reincarnation. But after hundreds of their patients revealing similar stories

---

[11] Henry, William. "Articles/Posts." William Henry Nashville. http://www.williamhenry.net/whblog/.

[12] "Dr. Michael Newton | The Founder of The Newton Institute." The Newton Institute. https://www.newtoninstitute.org/about-tni/dr-michael-newton/.

[13] "Founder: Dr. Ian Stevenson." University of Virginia Health System: Division of Perceptual Studies. https://med.virginia.edu/perceptual-studies/who-we-are/dr-ian-stevenson/.

under hypnosis, they couldn't deny the evidence. These doctors agreed that there is much more in play than just fanciful stories. Dolores Cannon and other respected researchers confirmed their findings as well. [14] The well known Edgar Cayce was also skeptical. He was a staunch Christian and struggled to come to terms with the contradiction between his understanding of Christianity and the information he consistently received in thousands of his self hypnosis sessions while accessing what are called the Akashic Records. These Records are like an "energetic storehouse" of all things that have happened, are happening, or will happen. Cayce was able to help thousands of people by accessing the Akashic Records. [15]

Karma

Compared to reincarnation, karma is a little more opaque for a lot of people. Karma simply means "action." More specifically, it is the way all imbalance is to be brought back into balance. Part of our reasons for reincarnating is to balance out actions we may have carried out in previous lives. Many in the West assume that karma is akin to payback, retribution, or "what comes around goes around." But this is not the true

---

[14] "Dolores' Career Biography." Dolores Cannon. https://dolorescannon.com/about/.
[15] "Edgar Cayce's A.R.E." Edgar Cayce's Association for Research and Enlightenment. https://www.edgarcayce.org/.

definition of karma or how the universe operates.

In *The Synchronicity Key,* David Wilcock gave a very interesting example of one balancing their karma. It comes from an Edgar Cayce reading which Cayce did on himself. Cayce had many previous incarnations on Earth but this one was especially moving.[16]

> The John Bainbridge incarnations are consistently the most surprising of the Cayce history of past lives, when seen in context with the historical figures he was also alleged to have been. At two different times in the 1700s he incarnated as an Englishman from the same family, and sailed to America to explore the new frontier. He was a gambler, womanizer, and a hard drinker, and he used his psychic abilities to cheat at playing cards as well as the shell game. Apparently he enjoyed this lifestyle so much that he reincarnated a second time to repeat the same self-serving behaviors. This accrued a great deal of karma, but his soul created an opportunity for him to

[16] David Wilcock, *The Synchronicity Key: The Hidden Intelligence Guiding the Universe and You* (NY, NY: Dutton, 2016), 161.

resolve it in the most dramatic way. At the end of his life there was a terrible famine. He could feel himself dying of starvation. He knew that the food he had with him was the very last he could find, and it wouldn't sustain him for long.

He noticed a child who was starving, a young boy, and had a complete heart opening of compassion for him. Bainbridge realized that if he gave the boy his food, the boy might have a chance to survive – or, at the very least, he wouldn't suffer as much. Bainbridge gave the boy the very last piece, for which the boy was extremely grateful and cried and Bainbridge cried as well. He died soon afterward. The Cayce readings spoke very fondly of this moment, saying that in this one gesture of selfless service, giving up his own life so that a younger person might live, he erased two lifetimes worth of negative karma.

To offer another example, let's say that John murdered Bill. While it is certainly possible that if John murders Bill, Bill may murder John in a different life, it is apparently not usually like this. Why?

Because then Bill will incur more karma. So there are many ways this can play out. In this example, it is possible that Bill will come back into an incarnation with John and need to take care of John, who may be handicapped or very sick his whole life. An example of this happened to my dear friend and mentor Toby Evans, who I have mentioned.

Toby was working on some maintenance on her rather large labyrinth that is cut into the tall prairie grass out in the middle of Missouri. Her husband, her sixteen year old son, and a friend of his were there helping. Up until that time, her son, being the teenager he was, just kind of giggled at the idea of his mom being a healer, Akashic Record reader, Shaman, etc. He did not believe in any of the witchy woman stuff. That day, Toby saw him from across the yard and, more than once, he started crying. His friend was subtly trying to console him. One moment, he would be fine, then crying again. Not wanting to embarrass him, she didn't address the matter until later in the day.

When Toby asked him, her son said that when he looked in the direction of their house, he would see the house about every other time. The other half of the time, he saw a scene from the 1800s where he and his dad were in Union soldier uniforms. They were tossing the bodies of dead Native Americans onto a wagon without a cover. The dad was a Union captain, and the son was a lesser officer, but Toby's son recognized both himself and his dad. When Toby used her skills to investigate, it turned out that Toby, in that previous life, was in the tribe of Native Americans they had killed. While she was able to escape, she lived a life of extreme sorrow and pain due to the loss of her people and her beloved life in general. So in the case of Toby's family, they all reincarnated together again so that the father and son could watch over Toby in this life. This is one of the many ways in which karma can be balanced or "paid back" (even if I am not fond of that term). Just as remarkable, the massacre took place on the same land Toby and her family live today. I have been on that land several times and before even knowing about this story, I was definitely getting the sense of the presence of Native Americans. Toby had a Shaman on the property who could actually see them. They are Osage Indians as was Toby in that life, and they are continuing to watch over her as well as her land they had once lived on together.

Pre-incarnate Choices

Working in tandem with karma, our souls choose certain lessons or ways to balance our karma. We (as souls) choose many things before incarnating into another physical body. This can be any of a huge number of things such as choosing the type of body we will have in this life, what race we are, where on the planet we will be born, etc. It can also be choosing, like above, to learn about forgiveness. Maybe we even want to experience what it is like to be a murderer or a victim. Maybe we choose to have a birth defect or health issue. Pre-incarnate choices can be just about anything. They can even be choosing to come in and be a rich and powerful person. Since, however, there is usually not a great deal of spiritual evolution in that, we may not choose that. If this seems a little strange, maybe it will help to look at it like this. Your soul has a plan before coming here into the physical realm. But once "you" (your conscious mind) enters the scenario, anything is possible. Free will is the absolute number one rule in the universe. If, on an increasingly conscious level, you are able to hear the Voice and start to remember who "you" truly are/were before coming here, everything changes. This is exactly what happened to me.

Many would ask, "Why would I want to have an unhealthy body or a birth defect? Why would I want to be the victim of a murder?" The answer is that "you" did not. Your soul did. The Soul has 100% free will as to what it wants to experience in its physical (and non-physical) lives. Our souls know that the physical realm is a type of school. It's even a type of playground. And after we leave the physical existence, we are once again all connected to the One. As always, there is a Divine Plan in place.

Soul Families/Soul Contracts

Pre-incarnate choices are not only made on an individual basis. We make agreements with other souls as well, known as soul contracts. (I prefer to call these soul agreements) These agreements can be made with one other soul or a group of souls. These are known as your soul family.

Before any of us came into this life (or other lives) we all make choices regarding the experiences we would like to experience and thus learn from. We chose our parents. We chose the date and place of our birth. These two choices have a great deal to do with what we are each choosing to work on in this life, known as our soul purpose. We choose the type of body we will have. We choose the people (souls) we think we will learn the most from. You know, those big lessons. The hard ones. The experiences that you felt like you would not get through but because you did persevere, you wouldn't have traded the experience for anything because it transformed you. If we learn what our soul wanted to learn from the situation, we are happy to have gone through it. If we were not happy to have gone through it, guess what? We haven't yet learned what we (our soul) wanted to learn. It is also possible to choose an easy life in which you would not have any big challenges, but the very fact is that even coming to earth means we will all face challenges if for no other reason than we are living behind the veil.

Let's go back to the example of wanting to learn about unconditional love and forgiveness. Before coming into physical, outside of linear time, and before coming into this illusion, you made an agreement with one or more of your soul family. (Members of your earthly family are not always the only members of your soul family.) Your asking them to help you learn about forgiveness means that these souls, once in your life here, agree to do things to you which would challenge you on the deepest level, things that are mean and seemingly unforgivable. If you were unable to forgive them, there is a lesson lost, and your soul just may decide to try it again in another life with the very same soul or group.

A soul group, or soul family, often numbers from ten to forty souls. Other trusted sources such as Edgar Cayce, ascertained that groups can be well into the hundreds, and even thousands sometimes happen. It is extremely probable that anyone with whom you struggle to get along with are a part of your pre-incarnate choices which your soul has a desire to learn more about.

On a more subtle but equally important note,

there are also bump contracts. This is a more brief encounter. This happens when we might meet someone whose soul was sent by our soul in order to bump us in a different direction. It is like getting us back on course, getting back on the path our soul is trying to get our little avatar to go. These can be as short as a glance, a one minute conversation, or other spans of time like a few weeks or months. Maybe we all have a memory of a conversation which was pivotal for us and caused us to change directions or view the world a bit differently. Those may have been a bump contract with another soul.

If we can look at our life from a larger perspective like this, we can start to understand just how much it is in the nature of the soul to be in service to others. Imagine someone asking you to help them learn about forgiveness. On the other side of the veil, where we are all connected to the One, where there is only Divine Love, you might be reluctant to do unloving things to someone in the next incarnation. But loving them so much also means you are happy to be in service to them and help them with what they are asking for. It can be a hard pill to swallow, but we all ask for this type of assistance, and since we are in service to others, we lovingly agree to help one another.

The Veiling Process

The veiling process is fundamental key for this chapter and the rest of this book. I actually consider this to be the most distinct understanding to our entire existence on Earth. It's the reason we spiritually stumble so much here and, again, it's done by design. Everything is in Divine Order.

Every single human being on Earth comes here having undergone the veiling process. The veiling process (or forgetting process) means that when we are born, we forget who we truly are. We forget where we came from – Spirit. We no longer remember our connection to Source, God, or Creator. However you define those terms, we come into a sort of spiritual deprivation tank where we have the illusion of being separate from everything and everyone. This is purposely done by separating the conscious mind from the unconscious mind, thus putting what many people would call the ego into place within us. At around twelve to fifteen months, a child starts to develop more and more self-awareness, and when this happens, the concept of self grows deeper and deeper into the illusion of separateness.

Millions of years ago, there was no veil. There was no separation between conscious and unconscious mind. But it was taking third-density beings forever to choose which way they wished to evolve. So the Logos (God, if you like) put the veil into place in order to greatly accelerate our spiritual evolution. If we came into physical knowing all there is and feeling the oneness of everything, we would not learn nearly as fast nor as deeply.

Having forgotten who we are means that we are living within an illusion deeper than our little ego minds could ever imagine. It is a bit like the holodeck on *Star Trek,* but to the infinite degree because those in the holodeck were actually aware that they were within an illusion. They were aware that it was real but also not real. Yes, your head will hurt when you walk into a door. (Or when you try wrap your head around this concept.) Your hand will feel pain when stung by a bee. Your toe will hurt when it finds the table leg in the dark. We will feel like our heart is breaking when we lose a loved one, yet all sources say this that it's not real. When we leave the earth plane upon the death of the physical body and go to higher planes, the veil is removed. And just like sick bay treated people who were injured while on the holodeck, our soul may need healing. The amount of healing varies, depending on how much trauma, if any, was experienced. But after the healing, we all realize, *Wow, it seemed so real but it wasn't.*

Channelers, mediums, those who open the Akashic Records, etc. have been piercing the veil since humans have been here. They also tell us that every single person on earth has these abilities. There is a growing number of us who are starting to understand that this gift has actually been tricked out of us by certain beings. This is one of the biggest reasons I was told to write this book, so that readers who are skeptical about these things might have a second look. Yet I know it's possible that most skeptics will need to be hit over the head with the metaphysical hammer like I was.

There is more great, exciting new for me as well since it seems that at this time on Earth, the veil is the thinnest it has been. There is an enormous spiritual awakening happening on our planet in the past decades. I know that it hit me like an avalanche even if the road leading to it was quite the challenge.

To close this section on the veiling process, in believing we are separate from one another, a great many number of lessons manifest throughout our day. Most of all, how we treat others. It is the veil which causes us the illusion. If I see you as me, then who can I harm? Buddha is quoted as saying "See yourself in others. Then whom can you hurt? What harm can you do?" For the Christian, Jesus said it in many ways such as, "Whatsoever ye would that men should do to you, do ye even so to them."[17] In other words, it's the Golden Rule. One of my favorite quotes on the idea of separation comes from Ramana Maharshi when he was asked how we should treat others. He simply said, "There are no others."

Channeling

In short, channeling is when one has the ability to connect to the other side of the veil. In channeling sessions, there will often be questions/answers but sometimes it's simply the higher dimensional being transmitting teachings, information, or concepts. It is easy to get caught up in the semantics, though, and when we focus on those, we are still "in the head" because in the end, it's just energy. Everything is energy in one frequency or another, yet from our third-density reality, most of us have a more challenging time consciously connecting to those energies due to the veiling process.

There are a couple of types of channeling. The first is when a person "clear channels." This is when the channel is very aware of what information is coming in. Their eyes can be open or closed, but they are aware of what they are saying. Most channels operate this way. The second type is trance channeling where a person will go into a trance, thus removing

---

[17] Matt. 7:12 KJ21

their conscious mind from the equation and let another being speak through their body. There are usually questions and answers in these sessions as well.

There are some Christians, as well as others, who believe that channeling is spiritually dangerous. There are indeed risks of connecting to higher-density beings who are less than benevolent. Carla Rueckert, who channeled *The Law of One*, was an extremely devout Episcopalian. She read from the Bible daily, prayed to Jesus and God, and sang in the church choir for all of her seventy-plus years. She was deeply devoted to her religious beliefs. Since she was a very skilled channel, she could receive communications from many beings/entities. Every single time she would start to receive a contact from a being, she would challenge it three times by asking it if it agrees that Jesus Christ is Lord (it is cosmic law that they cannot lie to a direct question). If the being did not reply with a resounding yes all three times, she would cut the contact. Carla was a perfect example that Christianity and channeling are not only compatible, but they are wonderful partners and provide a safety as she did.

Everyone channels whether we are aware of it or not. You are channeling when you suddenly wake up with the solution to a situation you didn't have the day before. Artists are constantly channeling when they create art, music, poetry, and more. Music and art are very powerful mediums for bringing in information. As I already mentioned, I composed many songs for years as well as music without lyrics. I was not a great songwriter. I was very good at vocal arrangements, though. I am a natural for that. Anything you have a natural knack for is you channeling spirit. You're just expressing it in a slightly different way than others do. When asked how he created so many beautiful compositions, the acclaimed composer Vangelis emphatically said that all the compositions are "out there" (while reaching his hand up then pulling it back down) saying that all he does is pull them down to the planet.

Those who channel can simply be bringing in information, or they can be connecting to a higher dimensional being, but it's all the same because there is only the One. A little clarification here: When referring to a higher dimensional being, this does not mean that they are better, smarter, etc. We are all on the same spiritual trek, yet the paths on this trek are infinite in variety and number. There are so many different choices each of us make in deciding what sort of things, what sort of lives we wish to experience before even coming to planet Earth. From the extensive reading I have done, it seems that most beings do not choose to incarnate. They prefer to not separate themselves from Spirit and choose an existence behind the veil. This is not too surprising because from all accounts, incarnating into physical presents extremely difficult challenges because of the veiling process. Sources such as Kryon, *The Law of One*, Q'uo, Dolores Cannon subjects (who were in hypnosis and connected to Spirit), and many more say the same thing – that they actually admire that we choose to incarnate. They often say that we are part of a special group who incarnate into physical, and this is a special service we in physical have chosen. I recently saw an interview with Regina Meredith in which she pointed out that Hermetic teachings said that the angels and archangels bow their head in humility to the human who has awakened themselves since they know we are behind that veil and it takes an extraordinary amount of effort and discipline to attain such awakening.

I have mentioned Dolores Cannon and Dr. Michael Newton. Both were very seasoned licensed hypnotherapists. Neither of them had any idea when they started doing this that they would discover what they did. Dr. Newton was a particularly hard sell but eventually he had to acknowledge that his patients were indeed connecting to their subconscious, which is the other side of the veil. Completely independently, they discovered that when a person is deep in hypnosis, they are then connected to vast universal information which they would normally not be able to access. Semantics aside, they are channeling Spirit, which is connected to everything. While deep in hypnosis, we are no longer bound behind the veil because the conscious mind is no longer separated from the subconscious mind.

So, there are many more beings on the other side of the veil than there are on our side. The vast majority are in service to the others who are always here, and they want to assist us. They cannot assist us, however, if we do not ask. Cosmic law dictates that no service can be offered where none is requested. So if you find this interesting, keep asking. Just know that nothing will happen if it's not in our highest good. In other words, if my Higher Self has other plans for me, then nothing I ask for that would go against that will happen. Higher Self is in the driver seat, as I have learned over the last few years.

Edgar Cayce is one of the most well-known figures when it comes to being able to channel information from Spirit. His technique involved his going into trance and accessing what are known as the Akashic Records, which are a well known term (again, semantics aside) for the repository of all information past, present, and future. Cayce was especially gifted in his work, yet as a Christian, he was very much at odds with this ability. He did not feel something like this should be possible, yet he did it and did it very accurately for thousands of cases. He was able to help thousands of people by accessing the Akashic Records. With so many people asking him for help, he overworked himself. He had been warned about overworking by Spirit (In this case, the beings known as the Lords of the Records) who watches over this information in order to ensure no information will be given which might interfere with our free will.

Wanderers

These are the souls from other star systems who have volunteered to incarnate on earth at this time in order to help raise the collective vibration of the population. (Wanderers are sometimes also referred to as Star Seeds.) Many sources have been telling us that earth's population has been stuck in a sort of karmic loop and unable to spiritually evolve. Wanderers have already evolved to higher densities (or dimensions).

There have been Wanderers on Earth for tens of thousands of years, but that they were very few in numbers. That number increased slightly around the Industrial Revolution. But when nuclear energy was used to destroy lives in Hiroshima and Nagasaki, a type of beacon went out to the universe. Earth was in trouble. Because of free will being the number one principle in the universe, no beings could come to earth and tell us what we should do. So an experiment was put into place. Souls from all over the universe(s) were asked who would volunteer to incarnate here in order to help raise the vibration of the planet. So even though Wanderers come here from higher densities, they must still go through the veiling process. In agreeing to come here and forget, they run the risk of not remembering why they came to begin with. (I know that this Wanderer forgot until "it happened," and I began to remember.) If this happens, they may get caught up in the lower density vibration here on earth and create more karma for themselves. For this reason, Wanderers are considered courageous or possibly foolhardy by non-physical beings. The Voice guided me to write this book for that reason, to help more of us remember or at least become aware of some things that we may not have been aware of before.

It has been found through channeling that the one known as Jesus was a high fourth-density being who was ready to graduate into fifth density but decided to come to Earth in order to help us learn about love. There have been several different waves of volunteers, or Wanderers, Star Seeds, etc. The first of the big waves started in the Fifties and Sixties. Many of the first wavers weren't, or are still not, crazy about being here. As you read, I was one of those. Thus drug addiction and other self destructive habits set in. When I recognized Rael's story of ETs, there was a slight echo of "home being out there in the universe." Yet when I learned about Wanderers, I remembered all the times I was asking myself as a child who I was and why am I here. I also realized that it wasn't the Midwest I wanted to leave as a kid. It was the planet.

The first wavers' job was to ground the energy which would pave the way – setting the stage for the second wave. The second wavers' role is just to be beacons, kind of like lightning rods or antennae for the brighter energies to anchor into the planet more. Dolores said that the second wavers are often in a type of conundrum. Their only job is to mingle in with everyone in order to just share their energetic vibration. Yet many from the second wave are a bit, though not so drastic, like the first wavers. They would prefer to not to go out. They would rather be at home. The third wave are those born in the Nineties and 2000s, and they came in at an even higher vibration. You can see videos of some of these kids on YouTube where they are having conversations with crystals and have little trouble piercing the veil unlike most of us. The veil is very thin for them, and if we listen to them instead of making them listen to us, we would all be a lot better off, as they came in to teach us.

As of the early Eighties, there were approximately sixty million Wanderers on Earth. As of the early 2000s, the number had gone up to one in seventy, which would make it 100 million.

Interestingly, in a recent Pamela Aaralyn session, Dolores gave a staggering number of two billion who are now incarnated here.[18] Corey Goode also confirmed this from his contacts with upper density beings that there are a surprising number of these types of beings now on Earth assisting us.[19] This gives me great confidence that things are indeed going well in the midst of all we see happening around us.

Carla Reuckert wrote a wonderful and expansive book for Wanderers or those who feel they are not on the usual Earth type – kind of spiritual misfits. *A Wanderer's Handbook* contains so much helpful information for those of us who "don't feel like we're from around here."[20]

If you find this book interesting, if it strikes a bell somewhere deep inside, maybe you are a Wanderer. I know that once I started remembering, I understood why I am here. I got back on board with my pre-incarnate choice, and I love it here now. Scott

---

[18] "Introducing Pamela Aaralyn." Pamela Aaralyn, Avatar of Grace. https://pamelaaaralyn.com/.
[19] "Corey Goode." Gaia. https://www.gaia.com/person/corey-goode.
[20] Rueckert, Carla Lisbeth. *A Wanderer's Handbook*. Louisville, KY: L/L Research, 2013. http://www.llresearch.org/library/a_wanderers_handbook_pdf/a_wanderers_handbook_unabridged.pdf.

Mandelker, Phd, devised a quiz you can take to see if you are a Wanderer or similar ET soul.[21]

To wrap up this section, I feel that incarnating on Earth at this time is an enormous privilege. As Toby said to me a couple of years ago, "There is a long line of souls dying to incarnate here, and you were ushered to the front of the line." I didn't get that at the time, but I do now.

Linear Time Does Not Exist

It can be hard to wrap our head around the idea, but all the above concepts can all be arranged easily between souls because linear time does not actually exist. Time is a construct put into place in order to facilitate our spiritual evolution. We are placed in the spiritual deprivation tank, and the illusion of time greatly condenses our lessons and accelerates our growth. While outside of the illusion of time, it is easy for souls to organize many things together "out there." How is that even possible? For one, *The Law of One* tells us that space/time is our physical existence, but there is also a time/space in the equation. Time/space is the metaphysical, in which there is no linear time. It tells us that time is a construct, or part of the illusion and the veiling process we go through.

---

[21] Mandelker, Scott. "The New ET Quiz." Scott Mandelker. https://www.scottmandelker.com/Articles/etquiz.html.

I don't get much of that either my friends, but every last resource of my two years of intense studies all say this. What I tell people is that I don't understand it, but I am remembering. I am recognizing more by listening to that faithful Voice. And it really will explain a lot as we move along in this book.

Free Will

This is of the utmost importance and may go deeper than first glance. Free will plays out though all of the above concepts and does not in any way contradict any of them. Your soul's free will is what brought "you" here and then at that point, "you" are on your own – alone and living behind the veil. You can listen to your soul or not. You can follow the Voice, deny it even exists (like I did for twenty-three years), or you can really not think about it much. But all things are permitted because you have free will.

Free will also has a great deal to do with our karma. Examples of violating free will include offering unsolicited advice, or trying to convince someone that our opinion is right and theirs is wrong. More examples would be trying to force someone to do something, through manipulation or coercion. War or conflict of any kind are among the most blatant examples. Yet all of the examples I mention here are ubiquitous on earth. Interfering with someone's free will means we will be trying to influence them to stray away from their chosen path. (also known as *dharma*) Many times this is done unintentionally, and we will see in the next chapter how this has greatly impeded humanity's spiritual evolution. But as always, there is no bad news. Our spiritual evolution takes as long as it takes. Once again, there are only happy endings.

Chakras

Chakras will be mentioned throughout the rest of this book, so let's give them at least some substance here. For most of us, chakras are kind of a nebulous concept. They were for me until I started feeling all that energy I mentioned going through them. They are one more thing that I didn't believe but do now.

Chakras are the seven major energy centers of the human body. There are many other "lesser" chakras, but for this book, there are seven. Here is a very brief explanation of what the first four are responsible for. I am using only the first four as these are the bulk of what we are doing here on earth, as I hope to explain. Keep in mind that the chakras cannot be separated from one another as easy as it looks. They all work together and can only be separated intellectually.

Root: Our basic needs such as survival and procreation. Our sense of feeling safe (or not) lives in this chakra. Fear of losing our life. And, in our modern world, money would be considered in this since it is necessary to survive.

Sacral: Likes, dislikes, attachment, addictions, aversions, etc. This also has to do with how we see ourselves in the world and how we begin to learn how to interact with others. This chakra also has to do with intimate sexuality, as opposed to primal, which would be the root chakra. Consider it as having a lot to do with your personality.

Solar Plexus: Our will and power stem from this chakra. Since they do, this also has a great deal to do with our self esteem – or lack of it. This chakra (though it is not solely responsible for it) is out of balance when we try to control others or be controlled by them.

Heart: Universal love and compassion are here. Not "I love you," but a universal love and compassion. It is loving those who are different from us

and what I call the F-Bomb –
forgiveness.

As these first four chakras have so much to do
with the upcoming chapters, I will leave it with these.
The upper chakras get into more of the spiritual and
esoteric aspects of us as human beings. An important
thing to say here is that the heart chakra is the gateway
from the lower chakras to the upper. We will see how
and why very soon.

So, at least temporarily, I ask that you assume
these things to be real as we go through the remainder
of this book. It would be surprising if you don't have
any questions regarding these, but hopefully they were
summarized well enough to get us through. There are
thousands of pages written on each of these concepts,
and there is a list of my favorite authors provided at
the end of this book.

Chapter 19
The Law of One

From 1981-83, Don Elkins, Carla Rueckert, and Jim McCarty brought this information in from Ra, who are a sixth-density social memory complex.[22] They are a group of millions of souls who think as one cohesive group. They still retain their individual identities, but there is no separation of thoughts between them. Separation only happens on this side of the veil. Through trance channeling, Ra was able to communicate and answer questions put forth by Don, Carla, and Jim.

The first way Ra defined the Law of One was in their first session with Don, Carla, and Jim when they said, "You are every thing, every being, every emotion, every event, every situation. You are unity. You are infinity. You are love/light, light/love. You are. This is the Law of One." (Light/love refers to the physical, and love/light is the metaphysical.)

Simply, there is only the One. Nothing else. We are all part of the One. Nothing exists other than the one infinite Creator, God, Source, or any other term you attribute to that which is, actually, beyond words. Originally, the one infinite Creator wanted to experience (thus understand) Itself in all of its infinite

---

[22] "L/L Research." L/L Research. http://www.llresearch.org.

variations. It sent out, in infinite supply, its creative force energy, thus creating the Logos. Logos is the universe itself (or multiverse, if that is the case). The logos then created the sub-logos, which are the galaxies. Galaxies created the planets, etc.

As is the case with many trance channel sessions and hypnotherapy sessions where subjects would be connecting to their subconscious minds, Ra had great difficulty using human language to communicate. We on Earth are in third-density. We use language to communicate. Fourth-density and above use only thoughts to communicate. The evolution upward through densities takes, from our perspective in the linear time illusion, tens of millions of years. Having graduated to sixth-density, Ra has not used language to communicate (again, from our perception of time) in hundreds of millions of years. Like all discarnate beings, they said that it is a very inadequate form of communication. Numbers are also awkward for them in that they only see the one infinite Creator in everything. (Jim McCarty humorously once said, "Ra has a hard time counting past one.") In other words, Ra does not see you or I as individuals. Everything, be it a person, a tree, an atom, a planet, a universe and everything else, is the One. We are only different aspects of the one infinite Creator, which is in the process of understanding Itself through every possible perspective. Depending on our background, it may seem like a foreign concept that neither you nor I exist, but that we are only one aspect of the Creator knowing Itself. It may take some time. That is part of the illusion caused by the veil. This is another reason for the the twelve-inch journey being so formidable, as the veil is what separates the head from the heart.

Anything other than the one infinite Creator is an illusion, or what Ra refers to as "distortions." The term simply refers to anything other than the One. Throughout my studies, all sacred, as well as hidden or suppressed teachings, taught the same thing. The very first distortion set into place by the one infinite Creator was free will. *The Law of One* states incessantly that free will is the absolute most important principle in the universe. It was put into place so that every seeming separate piece of Itself would go off on its own to experience Itself in as many variations possible. This would mean that no matter what that piece chooses to do, there is no right or wrong. This is because anything and everything that could possibly take place is completely valid. It is exactly what the Creator wanted to do in the first place. While one may see violence, deceit, and greed in the world and deem it as being bad, it is all completely acceptable on the grander scale. This may be hard to be comfortable with, but if we look at this from the karma perspective, sooner or later it will all be balanced.

The second distortion was Love. Ra went on to tell us that, "the act of free will upon love creates the third distortion, light." I meditate on this powerful phrase regularly. And this light brings us to the densities.

Chapter 20
Densities

Having defined free will, love, and light, we can now move to the next concept. Ra used the term "density," which refers to the amount of light a being is able to contain in any given stage of its spiritual evolution. The more dense the light a being is able to contain, the higher through the densities a being evolves.

A being evolves spiritually over eons upward through the densities. According to *The Law of One*, there are seven. Upon graduating from seventh-density to eighth-density, the octave is reached (as in a musical scale). At that point, a new octave begins. The inevitable result is that everything goes back to the one infinite Creator.

There are varying discussions on semantics and even disagreements regarding the term "density" being synonymous with the word dimension. Many esoteric teachings claim there are many more dimensions than seven. This could possibly be explained by Ra's teaching that there are sub-densities, sub-sub densities, sub-sub-sub densities, etc. within these seven densities, as well as octaves of densities past our own current octave.

It can help to see our spiritual evolution up through the seven densities correlating to the way the kundalini energy flows up the spine. As each chakra is freed from blockage, the energy flows up. The energy from the root chakra, if it is clear of blockages, travels up to the second chakra at the sacral level. If the sacral chakra is free enough, the energy travels up our spine to the solar plexus chakra, and so on. The chart below is how Ra explained the purpose of each density. It is not coincidental that these correlate very accurately with our chakra system. We are a micro of the macro.

The following chart summarizes the densities and what their purpose is.

Density	Purpose
First	Being
Second	Growth
Third	Choice
Fourth	Love
Fifth	Wisdom
Sixth	Unity
Seventh	Nothingness

One can only speculate how the next octave would be set up. As we on Earth are in third-density, we will focus more on the first three densities with some information on the fourth.

First-density is the density of "being." This density is the elements: earth, water, fire and air. The friction these have upon one another through wind, rain, volcanoes, etc. eventually creates a certain sense of awareness in these entities. After tens of millions of years, they reach a certain level of awareness. It is then that they "reach harvest" (or graduate) into second-density. Who or what harvests them/allows them to graduate? There are higher density guardians who watch over this process.

Let's take a brief look at that word "harvest" Ra uses. Not surprisingly, the same word is used in many ancient scriptures like the Bible and the Quran when referring to "end times," when the Earth would be reborn into a type of golden age or time of great peace – when there would arrive a new heaven on earth and similar prophecies. In other words, "end times" meant the end of third-density, moving into fourth-density positive, which is 100 times more harmonious than third.

Second-density is the density of growth. As stated, there are countless sub-densities within these major seven. Second-density ranges from single celled life up through plants, insects, and animals, all the way up through advanced primates. Second-density gradually evolves through different levels of group awareness. For example, a field of flowers, in mid second-density, would have a group awareness. Plants have less awareness than animals, but they have more than you may think.[23] Animals have a bit more awareness, but it is still a group awareness, the herd mentality. Some have called that a "group soul." Eventually, though, each will reach a certain level of self-awareness, and they will reach harvest into third-density, human. They will at this time, of course, begin at lower third-density.

Here's something for all the animal lovers reading. Giving your pets love greatly accelerates their self-awareness. Since love is the second distortion, the act of love upon free will creates light. Your pets absorb more and more of the light you send them. A being graduates/harvests upward according to the amount of light it is able to hold. When this reaches a high enough level, beloved pets reincarnate as a third-density being, human. Knowing this is comforting to me having lost two beloved cats over the

[23] Lanza, Robert, MD. "Are Plants Aware?" Psychology Today. March 11, 2017. https://www.psychologytoday.com/us/blog/biocentrism/201703/are-plants-aware.

last few years.

It's maybe no coincidence I write this paragraph today. In the Introduction, I mentioned one of my cats, Freddy. Throughout these months of writing, he continues to impede my writing by sitting on my desk, insisting on attention (light). Freddy went missing this morning. I can use this as an example of second-density beings becoming more and more self-aware. I didn't panic the first two hours in searching for him, but I became more concerned as I walked the neighborhood again and again calling his name. I walked and called sporadically for a total of five hours. The little squirt was having a good enough time that he was not wanting to come inside. He was in second-density mindset. He was not answering back like he often does, though I am quite sure he could hear me. He was happy to be roaming like a herd animal would. But when he needed me, he called because he knew I would come. The cheeky little guy finally called out, but only because of getting himself into a pickle he couldn't get out of on his own. Somehow he made it onto the neighbor's roof and couldn't get down. He is self-aware enough to call for my help when he needs it. Our pets learn that they can manipulate us to an extent in order to get what they want (attention, food, petting, etc.). I'm so sure that Freddy will make it to third-density that I sometimes call him Mr. 3-D.

Chapter 21
Third-Density and Polarization

In my continuing research, I came across something that helped me to clarify more. Absolutely everything is energy. Matter is energy. Sound and light are energy. And, thoughts and emotions are energy. Emily Maroutian's book, *The Energy of Emotions,* describes how we send/receive energy thanks to our emotions.[24] In it, Emily also explains how the law of attraction works. In Law of One terms, we can think of "energy" used in this quote as being synonymous with "light."

> Energy is the currency of the universe. When you "pay" attention to something, you buy that experience. So when you allow your consciousness to focus on someone or something that annoys you, you feed it your energy, and it reciprocates with the experience of being annoyed. Be selective in your focus because your attention feeds the energy of it and keeps it alive, not just within you, but in the collective consciousness

---

[24] Maroutian, Emily. *The Energy of Emotions: The 10 Emotional Environments and How They Shape the World Around Us.* Los Angeles, CA: Maroutian Entertainment, 2015.

as well.

This is a foundation for the remainder of this book, not only the example of being annoyed, but absolutely all thoughts/emotions.

In the previous chapter, we saw that second-density is the density of growth. We now get to third-density (our density), the density of choice. Ra told us that choosing our polarization is our only job here in third-density. We are here to, and we must, choose the direction (or polarity) we wish to evolve. There are but two choices. They are service to self (STS) or service to others (STO). It is important to understand here that one can graduate into fourth-density on either path, either fourth-density positive or fourth-density negative. Thanks to free will having been put into place as the first distortion, either path is acceptable. This is also fundamental as we move on.

Here's where the veiling process comes into play. Having forgotten our connection to the One, we arrive here in third-density in the illusion that we are separate from others. From the moments in childhood where we start to develop a self-identity, we begin our path of choosing service to others or service to self. The STO path means that we endeavor, and it is not often easy, to see our self as others, and others as self.

Simply put, we treat others as we would like to be treated.

To graduate to fourth-density on the positive STO path, one needs to be in service to others fifty-one percent of the time by the time their body dies. It does not mean we need to have done that for fifty-one percent of our entire life. It means to be in that percentage at the time of our leaving this life. We have our entire life to hone those skills. (Whew!) Serving others can be the smallest of things like opening the door for people, offering a genuine smile, and being sincere when asking someone how they are today. It can be letting a car in ahead of us. The smallest of examples go a long way.

Working the STS path, one needs to be in service to self ninety-five percent of the time. Considering the percentage is so high, this is much more than cutting off people in traffic, trying to get the best of someone on a financial transaction, or interrupting in daily conversations. It is done by dominating, manipulating, or intimidating others in order to get our own way. STS people are those who see themselves as separate from, and even better than others. To reach ninety-five percent, one will need intentionally to do a great deal of unloving things to others.

The beings who are able to reach ninety-five percent service to self (STS) are the extreme. Someone who is a psychopath, for example, has no care whatsoever if they hurt others. They think only of themselves. At best, they take care of their close-knit peers, but only because those peers protect them as well. They spend their life manipulating, controlling, intimidating, or anything else in order to gain more power over others, in order to get them to feed them their energy. They make people fear them and manipulate people to love them, etc. They do not see others as being equals. They seek only to do, get, or take what they want, and there are no limits on how to succeed at this. As we move in deeper here, this may seem to get a bit creepy, but know that, in the end, there is nothing to worry about.

This is a great place to point out that if we respond to STS beings with love, compassion, and forgiveness, we will not send them anything they want. It's only when we react with fear, disgust, anxiety, anger, etc. that we are then sending them what they desire. In those moments we might respond with fear, resistance, humiliation, etc., we are sending them our energy, our light.

If we wish to walk the STO path, it is good to remember that we can fall onto the STS path when attempting to convince someone we are right and they are wrong, or any time we insult or act condescending toward someone. When we judge ourselves to be on a higher moral ground than others and basically, any time we see ourselves as separate from others, we are moving towards STS. Now, we live on a planet that can be pretty aggressive, and this is likely why only fifty-one percent is needed on the service to others path. Furthermore, service to others does not mean that we should allow others to walk on us. It doesn't mean we should not stand up for ourselves. Third-density is a challenge, but these are the ground rules for the density of choice, the density where we commit to one path or the other.

We on the STO path here in third-density can certainly have our hands full in learning how to deal with STS beings on our planet. But there is opportunity here. We can consider this as our catalyst, or "grist for the mill," as Ra says. These are the moments we are faced with the opportunity to greet the situation with love and compassion, or, on the other hand, resistance. It is not our STO path to try and dominate those who are trying to dominate us. To be able to recognize the love in the moment and not try to exert our will over the other is actually a very strong catalyst for our spiritual growth. That is maybe the trickiest thing we are dealing with while wanting to polarize onto the STO path on earth.

On the other side of the veil, the vast majority of beings are in service to others. (Remember the soul contracts.) And even here on earth, those who choose service to others greatly outnumber those who choose service to self. Yet both accumulate more light as they climb the density spiral. Free will must remain in tact, so the STO beings in higher densities offer service to all of us here in third-density, so long as service is requested. This is done through our thoughts, prayers, and asking for assistance. People have been doing this for thousands of years by asking beings such as angels, or the likes, for help.

For those of us wanting to walk the STO path in third-density, our catalysts are those many forks in the road when we decide which way we wish to polarize. How do we respond every time we see someone asking for help on the street corner? Do we find compassion for them, or are we indifferent? How do we react when we see a car in our rear view mirror wanting to pass us. Do we move out of the way? Or do we justify ourselves by thinking, *I'm going the speed limit. They'll just have to deal with it.* We stay in the STO mindset when we listen to someone without trying to "fix" their problems, unless they are asking our advice, of course. (This is something I have had to work on.) How do we respond when confronted by a person who disagrees with our belief system? Do we try to convince the other person that they are wrong and we are right? We choose our path every time we have an opportunity to serve ourselves or serve others. There are more of these moments than one might imagine.

Now, it is true that we have to think of ourselves if we are to make a living and many other things in this life, and I think that's another reason why only fifty-one percent is required on this path. If we can think of the welfare of others that much of the time by the end of our life, then we will graduate into fourth-density positive. (It is also noteworthy to know that third-density equates to the third chakra, which is largely where our sense of will and power come from. We decide how we will use our power in this life. Do we use our will to help others? Or do we use our will to try to dominate them or force our opinions on them?)

It should also be said that if you are a seeker, if you search for truth and love for all, there is a very good chance that you are on the STO path.

Chapter 22
Spiritual Conspiracies

Upon arriving into the heart, what I discovered led me to believe that we have been lied to on the grandest scale imaginable. You may be asking yourself how conspiracy theories have anything at all to do with spirituality. The answer is that there has been what I would call, a spiritual disagreement of sorts going on here on earth for thousands of years. Some have called it a spiritual war. There are rabbit holes within rabbit holes here, so I will need to tightly compact the approximately 20,000 pages I have read and many hundreds of hours of interviews and lectures I have seen. Three years ago, I scoffed at such ideas and wrote them off as conspiracy theories. The twelve inches proved me wrong.

What I found was beyond most of our imaginations. I have uncovered enough evidence that I now fully believe that we have been lied to by those who have controlled our leaders in every field. These include, but are not exclusive to, history, education, science, astronomy, mathematics, medicine, energy, physics, and religion. I don't just mean lying politicians or religious leaders who cover up crimes of pedophilia here. In some cases, we have been misinformed. In some cases, we have been told bold-faced lies. Because of this, we are living within an illusion. The illusion is in place in order to keep humanity living in lower vibrational energies such as fear, anxiety, anger, separation, etc. Why? When aligning with those types of energies, our higher thinking abilities shut down. Our spiritual nature is suppressed. Our creativity is diminished and even used against us. Our Divine birthright of connection to the Divine is taken from us. We give away our power to leaders who have convinced us that we need them in order to be close to God, or that we need politicians to protect us from other countries. All these things keep us out of the Light. But let's try to bravely move ahead.

This is where things can appear to get pretty dark, but keep your eye on the end game. There is always a happy ending. The STS being who wishes to graduate to fourth-density negative walks an extremely devoted path. Ninety-five percent of the time is a huge investment in trying to dominate others. If you have not surmised it already, it is the STS beings who I said have been manipulating us for thousands of years. Every ancient religion has told of the spiritual battle taking place and darkness trying to eradicate the light throughout nearly the highest of spiritual realms.

According to *The Law of One*, nothing was originally omitted from being allowed to happen so long as free will was respected. This is absolutely fundamental to what we are talking about. Whether

STS or STO, either path is acceptable to the Creator. Through a being's spiritual evolution up the densities, neither path is "good" or "bad." Ra said,"The Law of One blinks neither at the light or the darkness." (To put this into terms that would resonate with traditional religions, God is indifferent to anything evil because He knows that everything and everyone will eventually return to Him.)

Ra likens the STO and STS paths to a battery. Both polarities are necessary in order to make the battery work. The STO offers. The STS receives. Using this battery analogy, we can also illustrate how the light referred to earlier comes into play. The act of love upon free will is light, and the STO being offers light (their energy) to others. On the other hand, the STS being tries to take the light from others, keeping it for themselves. It boils down to either love of self or love of others.

Keeping Emily's quote in mind, all of the leaders to whom we have been following have been disempowering us, taking our energy. This happens through empty promises or creating an illusory fear of another country, creating more fear and separatism. This also happens by creating and promoting political differences between people. Every time we are fighting over politics, we send energy up to those who desire it. Every time we think our country will be bombed, we're sending more to them.

Secret corporations control more than I could ever could have imagined years ago, until I did the research. Former employees of such corporations like Corey Goode, Emery Smith, William Tompkins and others have come forward. None of them knew each other until a few years after Corey first came forward. All three of them corroborated the other's testimonies after meeting. They tell us that they saw much more advanced technologies decades ago than in even today's public awareness. In Smith's case, these were medical technologies.[25] Smith also claimed to know of, and also helped to develop free energy technology.[26] He was also warned by the representatives of these secret corporations to not release any information on this. All three men also found they had both seen many things such as smart glass pads (like an iPad) as far back as the Eighties.[27] They also say the food replicators, like depicted in the *Star Trek* series, have

---

[25] Cosmic Disclosure: Medical Devices of the Future. October 30, 2018.
https://www.gaia.com/video/medical-devices-future.
[26] Advanced Energy Technologies Exist. July 15, 2018.
https://youtu.be/UwsNQMhcWkc.
[27] Global Galactic League of Nations, 22 Alien Genetic Experiments, and Secret Space Programs. October 28, 2017. https://youtu.be/7Kk1J2XNoBU.

been a real thing for many decades.[28]

This book would need to be much longer to get into all it could in this chapter, but I would like to go down just a couple of rabbit holes. The first one is regarding the fluoride put in drinking water. We have been told that the reason it is added to our water is that it's good for our teeth. Dentists have been taught so in college. But the colleges are also controlled by the same STS corporations. Again, we have been misinformed (sometimes outright lied to) about many things. What most people don't know is that Hitler had fluoride put in the drinking water of prisoners in the concentration camps.[29] Surely he wasn't concerned about the prisoners' teeth. The Nazis were, after all, removing gold fillings from prisoners' teeth among the other violent acts. They were obviously not concerned with the well-being of the prisoners. The reason the Germans did this was to alter the prisoners' mental health. Among other things, fluoride calcifies the pineal gland, the seat of your intuition and higher

---

[28] Replicator Technology/Corey Goode Interview with David Wilcock. July 21, 2016. https://youtu.be/iVM0BOkkUTI.

[29] Bowers, Becky. "Truth about Fluoride Doesn't Include Nazi Myth." PolitiFact. October 6, 2011. https://www.politifact.com/florida/statements/2011/oct/06/critics-water-fluoridation/truth-about-fluoride-doesnt-include-nazi-myth/.

thinking.

To go a little further down the hole here, Dr. Pete Peterson has worked for many secret corporations as well as the Reagan administration. President Reagan called him "Dr. Who" because he could solve any problem thrown at him. Regarding the topic of fluoride, Peterson told interviewers that there is a bottom feeding ocean fish whose liver oil was proven to be remarkable.[30] It is the skate fish, and I take this oil daily. Peterson cited experiments done on children in Europe just following WWII. This fish oil prevented any and all cavities. It completely eliminated them. He went on to say that it also completely prevents plaque from forming in the arteries as well. According to Dr. Peterson, fluoride and chlorine are what actually cause plaque to form in arteries.

The last rabbit hole I'll go down here touches upon two things. US companies such as Ford, General Motors and Standard Oil (now Exxon)[31] sold products

---

[30] Peterson, Pete, Dr. "Ratfish Oil." Ratfish Oil Blog. June 29, 2009. https://www.ratfishoil.org/ratfishoil-blog/44-ratfish-oil-dr-pete-peterson-june-2009.

[31] "The Treason Of Rockefeller Standard Oil (Exxon) During World War II." Archive. February 4, 2012. https://archive.org/stream/pdfy-eQ-GW5bGFH1vHYJH/Th

to Nazi Germany as well as the US.[32] As Corey Goode pointed out, "They didn't even sell it to us at a discount." Furthermore, Prescott Bush, the grandfather of president Bush Sr., was on the board of directors of corporations helping to fund the Nazis.[33] My point here is not political. My point is that we have been mislead. It's not presidents, congress, prime ministers, etc. who run countries. Multinational corporations do. The third-density STS beings running secret corporations, including the media, suppress the truth to manipulate us. They keep us living in an illusion of freedom and democracy when the truth is far from it. If it seems too much to swallow, I invite you to dig. Though many videos and information are still banned, there is an abundance of interviews with respected researchers and former insiders. I will offer a list of my favorite authors at the end of this book.

One might wonder how these third-density STS

e Treason Of Rockefeller Standard Oil (Exxon) During World War II_djvu.txt.

[32] Dobbs, Michael. "Ford and GM Scrutinized for Alleged Nazi Collaboration." The Washington Post. November 30, 1998. https://www.washingtonpost.com/wp-srv/national/daily/nov98/nazicars30.htm?noredirect=on.

[33] Campbell, Duncan. "How Bush's Grandfather Helped Hitler's Rise to Power." The Guardian. September 25, 2004. https://www.theguardian.com/world/2004/sep/25/usa.secondworldwar.

people on earth get away with so much. The reason is that they also request help from higher-density STS beings, just as we do with higher-density STO beings like angels, or whatever your particular beliefs are aligned with. As ancient religious texts taught, there are higher density "evil" (STS) beings just as there are "the good guys" in higher densities. The third-density STS people request things like more money or more power over others. The fourth-density STS beings are very happy to help. Because since the third-density STS being is purposely choosing the STS path, they are agreeing to serve the agendas of the fourth-density STS being(s) who help them amass power and wealth. The third-density STS being is then feeding their energy (light) up the ladder, so to speak. Think of it as a pyramid of power in place or a kind of spiritual, multi-level marketing system. Wherever there is a pyramid of power in place, there is STS.

Now, the way third-density STS (people) do in order to serve the fourth-density STS beings is to keep, as much as possible, humanity struggling, fighting, fearing, judging, etc. These are our political, corporate and even some religious leaders. While there are technologies which would alleviate all suffering and strife on earth, the third-density STS people who run those corporations, agree to keep the trouble going here on earth. The fourth-density STS beings are then in their favorite environment, receiving those lower vibrational frequencies. While you and I may thrive in a loving environment, those beings thrive on the opposite, because that is what they themselves are. If you've heard of the Law of Attraction, it is the same principle. If we continue to have conflicts, if we continue to suffer as a species and harm the earth herself, we are feeding our energy to the fourth-density STS beings. Manipulating us into those lower frequencies gives them what they need.

David Icke has been speaking about these STS beings for well over twenty years.[34] He calls them the archons, which is how Gnostic Christianity referred to them. Icke has pointed out that these STS forces, not being able to interfere with our free will, have manipulated our perceptions. Since our thoughts come from our perceptions, this puts us in a compromised illusion where we give away our Divine birthright power. The archons need us to be living in our heads, not our hearts. That's where the lower vibrations can exist.

I kept digging, and it became eerily clear. Though I would have laughed at the idea while in the RM, I now see there is an STS agenda in place. While these beings were ascribed different names in different religions, the top tier (mainly fifth-density, but early

---

[34] Icke, David. "Home." David Icke. https://www.davidicke.com/.

sixth-density as well) STS beings seem to be the very beings which ancient scripture warned about. They were known as Lucifer, Satan, Beelzebub, Belial, among other names. Muslims refer to Iblis or Shaitan (Satan). How could there be so many different names for one supposed "evil" being? Colin Joe Byrne, David Icke, and others explain the seeming confusion by pointing out that there was an entire group of entities known as the fallen ones.[35] Christianity referred to them as the Fallen Angels. These, my friends, are among the top of the STS pyramid.

[35] Harrison, Lisa. "Colin Joe Byrne - Time to Change." YouTube. February 12, 2017. https://youtu.be/Or29BozvivQ.

Chapter 23
The Fix

The previous chapter may sound like heavy stuff. But all we need to do, if we want to unplug from all of that, is to not feed it our energy. The beginning of this journey for me was when I flipped the switch from thinking about what I am against, to thinking about all that I support. I immediately felt lighter. We can be aware of the STS vibrations and choose to not participate if we try as much as we can to see the love in every moment. We can even view these STS beings as our catalyst for reflection in order to remind us that we are choosing to be in service to others. Besides, fearing or resisting is what STS beings like.

So unplug from the lower vibrations and plug into all the higher vibrational energies: kindness, unconditional love, compassion, and forgiveness. Remember, if we emit the higher vibrations, they don't like it. Most importantly, it is our way out of the illusion. Now, these feelings of compassion and forgiveness should include harboring the same feelings toward the cheeky STS monkeys who have been manipulating us by mixing in their lies with some truths as well. It might help to remember that they are beholden to those above themselves.

Another way to stay out of the lower energies is

to remember that either path is acceptable on the grander scale. We are here to choose STO or STS. We are here to choose what traditional religion has often called good or evil, service to self or service to others. To try to remember that we want to choose service to others, we increasingly unplug from anything that perpetuates the illusion of separation between us. Where does this begin? In understanding we have been misinformed, even lied to. Even those of us who did not have a deeply religious background may remember that the one called the devil is "the father of all lies." (I can't help but remember the guitar with the devil and Rev 20:10 quote that made its way into my hands in 1983.)

This leads us to some even better news. We have the ability to not participate in all the muck. Ra stated that by the time a STS being graduates into lower sixth-density, they can no longer maintain their negative polarity. When these beings are in fourth-density, they are evolving up through the density of love. But a being on the STS path is working the love-of-self path. Fifth-density is the density of wisdom. On the STS path, wisdom is more like cunning or conniving in order to control others. Up to this point, these beings see themselves as separate from others. Sixth-density, however, is the density of Unity, and the sixth-density STS being can no longer see themselves as separate from others. They have reached what Ra calls a "spiritual entropy." The STS being has no choice but to recognize the oneness with the One/God/Source. They have no other choice than to reverse their polarity because they are faced with the undeniable recognition that all things are a part of the One. Having said that, this is apparently extremely difficult for them, and they have enormous work to do. After all, by this point in their evolution, they have been on the STS path for hundreds of millions of years (in linear time, of course). But their work will be done if they want to evolve, and it is the nature of all beings to evolve.

So there are no worries, friends. In fact, the "current" STS beings want us to worry. If we worry, we give them what they want. They want us to be in the good fights and the bad fights. They live on the energy we produce when we have anxiety, or when Republicans and Democrats fight, and when we watch that nonsense on TV. They thrive when we feel we're not good enough. They take our light when we agree to participate in the illusion of being separate. They need these energies because, as in the law of attraction, these are the energies they are aligned with. Like draws like.

When we get to the point where we realize that we have been lied to, we start to understand that STS beings are doing this in order to keep us from connecting to higher vibrations. If we have the desire to turn the boat around, I would say that this is the main punchline. Do not confuse forgiveness with acceptance. Because when we do that, we are giving them tacit permission to continue what they have been doing all along.

From here on out, I try, as much as I can at this point having not believed in these things a couple of years ago, to connect some of the dots. Specifically, how the dots connected in my personal story. I know well that I am only seeing some of the dots. But I have apparently sufficiently been placed on the fast track to my remembering, thanks to the Voice.

Chapter 24
And the Raelian Movement?

This is a long chapter but it is, in my opinion, one of the major reasons it needed to be written. It now seems more than clear that the biggest pre-incarnate choice I made was being with Rael and the RM for those decades. Almost twenty-three years in a sea of rational thought, it was a desert of connection to Spirit. I actually defied and denied all forms of the mystical, the esoteric, and most of all, Creator Itself. My resignation from the RM was indeed my graduation. What ensued was the Dark Night of the Soul, for which I am grateful. I suppose it could also be argued, however, that my Dark Night of the Soul was having walked away from Spirit for those twenty-three years, then having returned home.

I would like to say this first. There are many beautiful teachings in the RM, teachings I still deeply support. However, I have discovered teachings I believe to be traps as well. If the reader is a current member of the RM, this book may even deepen your faith in Rael. Or it may provide a catalyst for something else. Because while there are indeed some wonderful teachings in the RM, I now know several fundamental teachings are false. I am not trying to change anyone's mind regarding Rael or anyone else. I don't have a horse in that race. I am actually extremely grateful to Rael and the hundreds of members with whom I served in the good fight. I also believe that those decades for me in that "spiritual deprivation tank" were undoubtedly necessary for my growth. I truly think my joining was a pre-incarnate choice. And the moment I resigned, I reclaimed my own personal power after having given it away for so long. Far be it from me to say that the reader may be stuck in a belief system which has dis-empowered them. All I can say is that I had no idea how much of my own power I had given away until I had the courage to find my resolve and walk away.

I should also state here that any conclusions I draw regarding the RM in this book are only my personal conclusions, in case anyone in the organization gets any ideas about a lawsuit. I remember how they think, as I was head of legal affairs for the North American continent for about ten years. I restate here that I am not anti-Raelian, nor anti-anything. I am pro-truth and I now know many things to be true now which Rael said, in his writings and in person, are false. Does this mean Rael was lying? I do not know, but as we go through this chapter I will offer solid evidence that I believe shows *someone* lied.

In chapter seven, we discussed the tenet held by Raelians that all the material in Rael's books was given to him by an ET who claimed to be Yahweh, which is the name of the Old Testament God. The RM believes that Rael is the only person on Earth to be in contact with ETs – especially the only one to be in contact with the Elohim, the group of humanity's true Creators. As I started studying *The Law of One*, I was very surprised at some similar details contained within this material. What Rael had said in his books point to deception in the contact with the Elohim. If it were the case that Rael made the whole thing up, he somehow pegged a surprising number of details in *The Law of One*, which I would find miraculous.

One of the first things that caught my attention was in the Introduction to *The Law of One*. In Rael's book, the ET representing the Elohim allegedly told him that if a person wishes to increase their chances of telepathic contact with the Elohim (and telepathy in general), they should grow their hair long. The hair acts as antennae. In the opening pages of book one of *The Law of One*, there are some photos which show how Carla was lying in a very specific way that Ra requested in order to maximize the efficiency of the contact. Her long brown hair was spread across the bed. The caption indicated that the hair acts as antennae for the channeling contact. The same information is also mentioned in session sixty-nine, August 29, 1981.

Note: Any added parenthesis in the quotes from Ra are my additions in order to clarify what may otherwise seem unclear. The session number is listed, followed by the question number within the session. The Law of One material is free to view online.[36]

69.0 Ra: At this particular working (session) there is some slight interference with the contact due to the hair of the instrument. We may suggest the combing of this antenna-like material into a more orderly configuration prior to the working.

The much more pertinent similarities are those regarding Yahweh. Rael claimed that he had the face to face contact with an ET who claimed to be Yahweh. This ET said he was the head of the Elohim (a group of ETs) and said that he had presided over the creation of all life on Earth, doing this through a mastery of genetics. The information that unfolds in the rest of this chapter gets to be very interesting regarding this.

When referring to Confederations below, Ra is referring to groups of higher density STO beings who reach out to help us if the help is requested. This can be done consciously as in prayer or unconsciously

---

[36] "The Law of One." The Law of One (The Ra Material). https://www.lawofone.info/.

when enough people are wishing there was someone or something who could help them. This call for help can be of STO or STS depending on the polarity of those who call for help. But STS calls for help do not go to the Confederation.

18.14 Questioner: Can you tell me how Yahweh communicated to Earth's people?

Ra: I am Ra. This is a somewhat complex question. The first communication was what you would call genetic. The second communication was the walking among your peoples to produce further genetic changes in consciousness. The third was a series of dialogues with chosen channels. (Referring to telepathic contact.)

18.15 Questioner: Can you tell me what these genetic changes were and how they were brought about?

Ra: I am Ra. Some of these genetic changes were in a form similar to what you call the cloning process. Thus, entities incarnated in the image of the Yahweh entities. The second was a contact of the nature you know as sexual, changing the mind/body/spirit complex through the natural means of the patterns of reproduction devised by the intelligent energy of your physical complex.

I interject here that Rael claimed the Yahweh he met said that the Elohim did not create us with a soul, but that we do have access to eternal life through our genetics and an advanced form of cloning.

18.18 Questioner: Can you tell me Yahweh's purpose in making the genetic sexual changes?

Ra: I am Ra. The purpose 75,000 years ago, as you measure time, was of one purpose only: that to express in the mind/body complex (second-density beings, most likely apes) those characteristics which would lead to further and more speedy development of the spiritual complex. (speeding its evolution to third-density, or human)

18.19 Questioner: How did these characteristics go about leading to the more spiritual development?

Ra: I am Ra. The characteristics which were encouraged included sensitivity of all the physical senses to sharpen the experiences, and the strengthening of the mind complex in order to promote the ability to analyze these experiences.

18.20 Questioner: When did Yahweh act to perform the genetic changes?

Ra: I am Ra. The Yahweh group worked with those of the planet you call Mars 75,000 years ago in what you would call the cloning process. There are differences, but they lie in the future of your time/space continuum and we cannot break the free will Law of Confusion. (Meaning Ra will not give any information which might affect our karma, our free will, our choices in the future.)

If we take Ra at their word, this would mean that the Yahweh group transferred souls from Mars to Earth. This Mars story is recounted several times in *The Law of One,* so it is unlikely to have been a miscommunication. Through their own violent actions, the population of Mars (of approximately two billion), had destroyed their atmosphere while they were still in third-density. Upon their deaths, they were reincarnated onto Earth, relocating here in order to continue their third-density evolution.

The Ra group spoke many times of the Orion group who are of fourth-density STS orientation and who try as much as possible to skirt the law of free will. These STS beings, the vast number of whom originate from the Orion star cluster, are clever. Since they can't break the law of free will, they will try to manipulate us into using our own free will against us.

Ra stated that the Orion group came to Earth around 3,600 years ago in order to negatively influence and pollute the attempted benevolent STO actions of the original Yahweh group many thousands of years earlier. Don asked some questions regarding this.

16.15 Questioner: Can you tell me the origin of the Ten Commandments?

Ra: I am Ra. The origin of these commandments follows the law of negative entities (STS beings) impressing information upon positively oriented mind/body/spirit complexes. (People) The information attempted to copy or ape (mimic) positivity while retaining negative characteristics.

16.16 Questioner: Was this done by the Orion group?

Ra: I am Ra. This is correct.

16.17 Questioner: What was their purpose in doing this?

Ra: I am Ra. The purpose of the Orion group, as mentioned before, is conquest and enslavement. This is done by finding and establishing an elite ("leaders" of sorts) and causing others to serve the elite through various devices such as the laws you mentioned and others given by this entity.

16.18 Questioner: Was the recipient of the commandments positively or negatively oriented?

Ra: I am Ra. The recipient was one of extreme positivity, thus accounting for some of the pseudo-positive characteristics of the information received. As with contacts which are not successful, (when the STS Orion group is able to pollute the original good STO intent of information) this entity, vibratory complex, Moishe, (Moses) did not remain a credible influence among those who had first heard the philosophy of One and this entity was removed from this third-density vibratory level (his physical body died) in a lessened or saddened state, having lost, what you may call, the honor and faith with which he had begun the conceptualization the Law of One and the freeing of those who were of his tribes, as they were called at that time/space.

In other words, the STS beings gave pseudo positive information with enough negative information to sufficiently contaminate it. This is done in order to create an elite, a leadership which would be further up the STS pyramid. Another of the things here indicating STS influence is that they made laws. Laws violate free will.

I personally believe that it is likely that Moses, extremely positive himself, was deceived by an entity masquerading as Yahweh. Upon Moses' transitioning from the physical body, he needed to spiritually heal from the trauma caused by the deceit perpetrated upon him by the Orion group.

16.19 Questioner: If this entity was positively oriented, how was the Orion group able to contact him?

Ra: I am Ra. This was an intensive, shall we say, battle ground between positively oriented forces of Confederation origin and negatively oriented (STS Orion) sources. The one called Moishe was open to impression and received the Law of One in its most simple form. However, the information became negatively oriented due to his people's pressure to do specific physical things in the third-density planes. This left the entity open for the type of information and philosophy of a self-service nature.

Ra says that there have been many channels who start out by receiving a positive STO connection, but, if the channel starts asking transient questions (questions that are not of a spiritual nature), the positive connection will weaken. When that happens, the STS being is all too happy to emulate that positive being and will start offering less and less truth. The STS being will sometimes also offer specific "gloom and doom" prophecies. None of these come true, and the person receiving the information is discredited. Again, however, the STS and STO only respond to the call. In this case both the STS and STO are abiding by the rules. Don then asked something very important.

16.20 Questioner: It would be wholly unlike an entity fully aware of the
knowledge of the Law of One to ever say "Thou shalt not." Is this
correct?

Ra: I am Ra. This is correct.

Any commandments of any kind are a direct infringement upon free will. Even the word "should" is an infringement because we are telling someone what to do and so are infringing on their free will. In the above text, we see that laws are the same thing. In our lives, we are all so accustomed to many laws. Speed limits may not seem like huge infringements, but others are. Laws such as taxation definitely set up an elite further up the STS pyramid, as well as those who serve the elite, who are keeping us as partially free slaves. Many of our biggest laws come directly from the Ten Commandments. This is one of the ways in which we were subtly tricked so long ago that most people have not been able to follow the flowchart back to the culprits. Moses had indeed grasped the Law of One, yet STS beings were able to confuse things. These commandments further violated free will because they interfere with one's polarization (as well as one's karma, which is up to the person to work out without any outside influence). They impede one's spiritual progress because we are in third-density to choose our own path. This is one of the ways we will see later how humanity's spiritual evolution has been impeded.

While on the topic of laws, we can also look at the societal norms and rules. These are simply a different type of law which are enforceable not through legal means, but through our peers. We can see examples of these everywhere. Wherever there is a feeling of being separate from another, superior or inferior, we can find its roots in STS. In the case of feeling superior to someone else, we are placing ourselves in the position of the elite, feeling more powerful than someone else. On some level, we are demanding them to give us the respect that we are not giving them. We are then taking their light, or taking their energy. When feeling inferior to another, we are sending our light/energy up the STS pyramid. Racism is a clear example of this. Another widespread example on earth is when one believes their religion to be good while feeling another's to be inferior. And while the draft was abolished in the US decades ago, there is still a national pride that inculcates us with the idea that one country could be better than another. All the leaders have to do is tell us that the people on the other side of the world are trying to make us submit to them through one sort of force or another. All three of these examples have lead to millions of deaths while people were trying to control or manipulate others into submitting to them. Feelings of superiority, inferiority, fear, distrust of others or anything which separates us has its origins in STS.

In a different session, Ra gave more information on Yahweh and his genetic experiments. The real Yahweh had genetically created the race of people who would eventually be living in the Egyptian area. It's no stretch at all to assume these are the people who were led by Moses. Ra went on to say that the STS Orion entities were able to tell these people that it was Yahweh who gave the Ten Commandments, but it was actually an Orion STS entity masquerading as the real Yahweh.

> **24.6 Ra:** An entity of the Confederation, many, many thousands of your years in the past, the one you may call "Yahweh," had, by genetic cloning, set up these particular biases among these peoples who had come gradually to dwell in the vicinity of Egypt, as well as in many, many other places, by dispersion after the down-sinking of the land mass Mu. Here the Orion group found fertile soil in which to plant the

seeds of negativity, these seeds, as always, being those of the elite, the different, those who manipulate or enslave others.

The one known as Yahweh felt a great responsibility to these entities. However, the Orion group had been able to impress upon the peoples the name Yahweh as the one responsible for this elitism.

Once again, free will is paramount. No STO being would ever give commandments. Only an STS being would do this. In this case, they did it by using the people's free will against them by posing as the Yahweh they loved and respected. In other words, that belief system was then corrupted.

To set up the next quote better, Ra had mentioned that the real Yahweh had originally tried to offer the Law of One to the people mentioned here.

24.9 Questioner: Then (the real) Yahweh, in an attempt to correct what he saw as what I might call a mistake (I know you don't want to call it that), started 3,300 years ago with the positive philosophy. Were both the Orion and Yahweh philosophies impressed telepathically, or were there other techniques used?

Ra: I am Ra. There were two other techniques used: one by the entity no longer called Yahweh, (who now went by another name after having his name hijacked) who still felt that if it could raise up entities (create people) which were superior to the negative forces, that these superior entities could spread the Law of One. Thus this entity, "Yod Heh Shin Vau Heh," came among your people in form according to incarnate being and mated in the normal reproductive manner of your physical complexes, thus birthing a generation of much larger beings, these beings called "Anak."

I could be wrong, but I assume the above is referring to Genesis 6 story of the sons of Elohim mating with the daughters of men. (Which Rael also said his Yahweh told him.) The Nephilim named in the Bible were giants, which, when mating with smaller humans, would then produce larger offspring than before.

Ra (cont): The other method used to

greater effect later in the scenario, as you would call it, was the thought-form such as we often use among your peoples to suggest the mysterious or the sublime. You may be familiar with some of these appearances.

Ra refers here to "thought forms." These are images which are indistinguishable from any other thing we would see here in third-density that would leave impressions on us. Things such as UFOs, people, ETs, holy visions, or any image we might find inspiring. In fact, Rael's book states that the ET he met said that they sometimes cause us to see things, and they sometimes even find it amusing.

24.10 Questioner: Could you state some of those [thought form things]...?

Ra: I am Ra. ...the so-called wheel within a wheel (Ezekiel chapter one) and the cherubim with sleepless eye.

The opening of the Ezekiel scripture is probably the most used of all Biblical texts as evidence for UFOs in the Bible. Rael also claimed the ET he allegedly met also quoted the opening part of Ezekiel as well, which describes the "wheel within a wheel," or a UFO.

The Orion group doesn't stop after successfully "interrupting things" as they did by using the name Yahweh. If transient questions are asked, the positive communication will eventually cease, and the STS beings are very happy to step in, mimic the positive entity, and pollute the information more and more.

24.16 Questioner: …could you tell me if you're saying the Orion group was successful in polluting, shall we say, some of the positively oriented prophets with messages of doom?

Ra: I am Ra. This is correct…

The original subtitle to Rael's second book was originally something to the effect of, "The end of the world through nuclear disaster is soon. They (the ETs) will come to save the just." There were also other regular warnings of doom in Rael's writings as well as may of his speeches, although mixed with quite benevolent ideals. The reason the Orion group give messages of doom is to discredit the person when the events fail to take place.

Another interesting example of this type of mixed information is from session twelve. Ra is explaining that the Earth is in quarantine in order that its people's free will not be impinged upon.

12.7 Ra: The Creator is one being. The vibratory level of those able to reach the quarantine boundaries is such that upon seeing the love/light net it is impossible to break this Law. Therefore, nothing happens. No attempt is made. There is no confrontation. The only beings who are able to penetrate the quarantine are those who discover windows or distortions in the space/time continua surrounding your planet's energy fields. Through these windows they come. These windows are rare and unpredictable.

12.8 Questioner: Does this account for what we call the "UFO Flaps" where a large number of UFOs show up like in 1973?

Ra: I am Ra. This is correct.

(I remind us here that Rael claimed that his UFO/ET contact was December 13, 1973.)

12.9 Questioner: Well then are most of the UFOs which are seen in our skies from the Orion group?

Ra: I am Ra. Many of those seen in your skies are of the Orion group. They send out messages. Some are received by those who are oriented towards service to others. These messages then are altered to be acceptable to those entities while warning of difficulties ahead. This is the most that self-serving entities can do when faced with those whose wish is to serve others. The contacts which the group finds most helpful to their cause are those contacts made with entities whose orientation is towards service to self. There are many thought-form entities in your skies which are of a positive nature and are the projections of the Confederation. Other sightings are due to the inadvertent visualization by your peoples' optical mechanisms of your own government's weaponry.

Once again, if we can take Ra at their word, then the Orion group may have contacted Rael with a message he would find "acceptable," yet polluting the information with several warnings of difficulties ahead.

Let's look now at other similarities, specifically

regarding STS. There are five Raelian Commandments, and we just discussed the idea of commanding anyone to do anything is a direct infringement upon their free will. The first Raelian Commandment is that all who believe the information in Rael's book officially join the RM by transmitting their genetic code to them as I described. They also commanded that people give 1% of their annual income to Rael and to spread their message to all of humanity so that the embassy can be built. In 1992, these seemed very small things to ask. After all, I loved and respected the Elohim (and I still do love the true Elohim and true Yahweh) but once again, if we look at any commandment in terms of violation of free will, things get fishy quickly.

Below is another quote from Ra regarding fourth-density STS beings polluting what may have begun as positive channels or messengers. First, there are three things to keep in mind.

1. Rael has always claimed that he is in telepathic contact with the beings who told him they are the Elohim, and specifically Yahweh.
2. Fourth-density STS beings sometimes create thought forms that may appear as very real, in this case, UFOs and ETs in order to manipulate who may otherwise be well-meaning people.
3. When I asked Kim in 2016 if Rael was really in

contact with the ETs, her answer was, "He's in contact with them telepathically, not physically."

Ra: Nearly all positive channels and groups may be lessened in their positivity or rendered quite useless by what we may call the temptations offered by the fourth-density negative thought-forms. They may suggest many distortions towards specific information, towards the aggrandizement of the self, towards the flowering of the organization in some political, social, or fiscal way.

In my view, this is very much what happened with the RM. Ra says that any channel (or telepathic contact in this case) and the channel's group (the RM) was led to an STS path by self aggrandizement, the spreading of the RM in a political, social, and fiscal way. These things create separation.

There are many things in the RM that I now personally believe wreak of fourth-density STS beings at work here. Some of these are the following:

- The ET telling us that we do not have a soul.
- The good fight, thus perpetuating separation.
- The pyramid of the Raelian organization.

- Inner politics causing more separation.
- The doomsday warnings.
- Teaching Raelians that they are "special" because they recognize the Elohim (Elitism).
- Rael saying the ET told him there are no such things as negative ETs.
- The Jewish race being superior to others (Elitism).
- That the most devoted Raelians being among the first to attain eternal life (Elitism).

I could list many more examples of Ra saying what Rael claims to have been told, and this makes be believe it is very likely that Rael was indeed contacted by either an ET or possibly a "thought form ET." Of course, there is a possibility that he made the story up as well but if he did, he did so with a surprising amount of coincidences to the Ra material.

You may remember that the moment I resigned from the RM in November 2014, I felt an extreme lightness upon sending the email, when I thought at the time it would bring a heavy heart. While I definitely went through a considerable healing time of about eighteen months through my Dark Night of the Soul, I actually believe that this was the plan all along. I now understand that my Higher Self actually wanted to experience what might be called a "veil behind the veil," meaning that I would not only be living behind the veil we all live here in third-density, but I would go even deeper and even deny the existence of Source. After the lesson was learned, my Higher Self was finished with that experience. Eventually, I was able to hear the Voice that told me, *Okay. We're done here. Let's move on.* The lesson was learned, and it was time for me to reclaim my own power, reclaim my freedom. My freedom upon resigning was wonderful even if it was foreign for some time. And the eventual freedom I achieved after the first fourteen months in KC was beyond what I could have ever imagined.

We see a lot of religions and other leaders on Earth who teach that there are commandments that must be followed, one group is right and the other wrong, or their followers will be rewarded and others will not. Whether the leaders know it or not, and I believe the majority do not, they are toeing the line of those negative fourth-density STS beings. But there are also many leaders, the elite, who indeed know very well who they are serving. I'll go into more detail on that soon.

Here are other very interesting examples which Ra gave regarding the Orion group infringing upon free will and thus manipulating people in order to enslave them. The first is from session sixty.

60.17 Questioner: Thank you. I don't

know if this question will result in any usable direction, but I think I must ask it. What was the Ark of the Covenant, and what was its use?

Ra: I am Ra. The Ark of the Covenant was that place wherein those things most holy, according to the understanding of the one called Moishe, (Moses) were placed. The article placed therein has been called by your peoples two tablets called the Ten Commandments. There were not two tablets. There was one writing in scroll. This was placed along with the most carefully written accounts by various entities of their beliefs concerning the creation by the One Creator.

This Ark was designed to constitute the place where from the priests, as you call those distorted towards the desire to serve their brothers, could draw their power and feel the presence of the One Creator. However, it is to be noted that this entire arrangement was designed, not by the one known to the Confederation as Yahweh, but rather was designed by negative entities preferring this method of creating an elite called the Sons of Levi.

If you're following what Ra is saying, these service to self beings are very clever in the way they manipulate us into using our own free will against us. Whenever a hierarchical system is put into place, we will have a system of STS. This is true in religions. Priests answer to bishops, who answer to cardinals, etc. It is my personal opinion that the Vatican is one of the biggest examples of STS. Even on the surface, they have billions of dollars, real estate, and priceless treasures, yet they recommend poverty and humility. Instead of exposing and prosecuting the pedophiles within their pyramid of power, they protect them. How could this be?

Once the STS entities had people on Earth who had asked for their assistance, they had a foothold here. The STS entities operate like the typical corporation pyramid which is always service to someone further up the ladder. Just look at what corporations have been doing to our planet for the past 65 years.

On a side note here, Ra stated in two different sessions that President Eisenhower was contacted by the Confederation. The Confederation, of which Ra is a part, is a large group of beings from various densities, in service to the Earth's populations who are requesting assistance.

24.19 Questioner: It's not too important, but I would really be interested to know if Dwight Eisenhower met with either the Confederation or the Orion group during the 1950s or that time?

Ra: I am Ra. The one of which you speak met with thought-forms which are indistinguishable from third-density. (Thought forms) This was a test. We, the Confederation, wished to see what would occur if this extremely positively oriented and simple congenial person with no significant distortions towards power happened across peaceful information and the possibilities which might append therefrom. We discovered that this entity did not feel that those under his care could deal with the concepts of other beings (ETs) and other philosophies. Thus an agreement reached then allowed him to go his way, ourselves to do likewise; and a very quiet campaign, as we have heard you call it, be continued alerting your peoples to our presence gradually. Events have overtaken this plan.

So it seems Eisenhower didn't think people would be able to handle the disclosure centering around UFOs, ETs, etc. More interesting, however, is that there were no other attempts from positive beings in the previous eighty years from 1981 (the time of the session) which would put us around 1900. Don continued.

> **26.33 Questioner:** Then are all of the landings that have occurred except for the landing when Eisenhower was contacted, are all of those landings of the Orion group or similar type groups?

> **Ra:** I am Ra. Except for isolated instances of those of, shall we say, no affiliation, this is correct.

I believe this to be a very important point regarding Rael's Yahweh. All landings in those eighty years were from the STS negative Orion group. This places one more piece of evidence in the file that Rael was contacted by a "False Yahweh." A negative entity using Yahweh's name would be a very clever way to manipulate us, and has been done before as we have seen. Yahweh's name has held an extremely large amount of energy as this name was deeply revered to hundreds of millions of people over thousands of years. The peoples of 3,000 years ago strongly believed that there was a great power in words in and evoking a god (or God) should be taken very seriously and was not to be done lightly. Since we get who we call for when it comes to STS or STO, maybe we now know why.

There is also another reference in the Law of One to Eisenhower. According to the former insiders, these are corporations that work with the military. This is referred to as the Military Industrial Complex (MIC). Respected researcher Dr. Michael Salla interviewed a former CIA agent on his deathbed.[37] His story was compelling. He told of a story in 1958. President Eisenhower had just gotten wind of Area 51, a top secret military base at the time. The president wanted to receive information on extraterrestrials said to have been on the base. His request was ignored. One would think that the leader of the free world would be able to receive a reply. The reason was that the base was controlled by at least one secret corporation, and the military was protecting their interests. Having been ignored, Eisenhower sent back a message threatening

---

[37] Salla, Michael, PhD. "Eisenhower Threatened to Invade Area 51 Former US Congress Members Hear Testimony." ExoPolitics. May 03, 2013.
https://www.exopolitics.org/eisenhower-threatened-to-inva de-area-51-former-us-congress-members-hear-testimony/.

to use the army to invade the base. Only then was he was invited to visit. What he saw apparently shocked him because as a result of his experience, he warned of the dangers of the Military Industrial Complex in his farewell speech on January 17, 1961.[38] If you watch this speech, you can begin to leave behind the conspiracy theories and journey toward the facts. They may seem unnerving at first. But I would personally rather have the truth, no matter how ugly, than believe a lie, which I see now has been the case for humanity for a long time.

The following is also a very important point when we remember that the STS beings cannot infringe upon free will but that they can manipulate us into giving up our free will. Rael said that the ET he met told him that the Elohim (group of ETs) said that they would like to officially return to interact with us and share their technology but that we would need to invite them. Sharing their technology is exactly what some of the fourth-density STS beings have been doing in giving technology to 3D STS people here who are polarizing toward STS. The 3D STS people here on earth are keeping us in the lower vibrational frequencies. They're keeping us in wars and struggling to make a living as we referred to earlier.

---

[38] "Eisenhower Farewell Address." YouTube. May 17, 2015. https://youtu.be/OyBNmecVtdU.

This may help to understand why the 4D and 5D STS negative beings do what they do. There are Gnostic scholars who say that the archons (also known ad fallen angels) are higher density beings who had purposely disconnected themselves from their original Divine connection. This would in no way contradict the idea that the one infinite Creator chose to split Itself into an infinite number of pieces, instilling free will in order to experience Itself in all possible ways. After all, free will is free will. Either path is acceptable.

All STS beings, no matter their density, are afraid that humanity will wake up to our true potential because if we do, they will lose the source of the energies they take from us. The varied assortment of energies of harm we cause to ourselves and our environment are their food source. This food energy is also referred to as "loosh", a word most believe is a derivative of the word "Lucifer". But, as always, there are only happy endings. We will all eventually go back to source. We will all go back to the One, to God, or however you define the one thing that is indefinable.

The last question I would propose brings us closer than ever to Source, God. And there are sources I have read which lend merit to this. What if the upper-density STS beings have, all along, been performing actual STO work here in doing what they are doing? Very much like the idea of soul contracts, these beings may have even agreed to play a certain "black hat" part in the Divine Plan. In doing all they can to be STS, be manipulative, cruel and diabolical, they give you and I the opportunity to choose service to others. After all, our third-density is the density of choice. Which will we choose?

Living as we are behind the veil in third-density means that it is almost impossible to know for certain exactly what is going on on either side of the veil - or even this side of the veil. We are living in an illusion purposely designed to accelerate our spiritual evolution. Yes, our perceptions of reality here on this side of the veil are sometimes influenced by fourth-density STS beings, who are in cahoots with third-density STS people on earth who are trying to work their way up the STS pyramid. But we also have fourth-density (and higher) STO beings who are there for us, so long as we ask for assistance. Our third-density experience here is, once again, about choice. This is the purpose of the design. Being separated from the All that is/God/Source, we have no choice but to live on faith, no matter which polarity we are choosing.

There is more good news. There is a huge awakening taking place on this planet, and we on the STO path are tipping the scales. More and more of us are "remembering". The STS beings, terrestrial or not, know it. This is the reason the Voice told me to write this book. It told me to get this information into the collective consciousness. If we can do that, it's over for STS beings on earth.

Of course it's up to us if you believe anything I have written up to this point. Please use your own discernment. I didn't believe any of this until I kept digging. If you're interested, dig. And for the final time, I say here that in the big picture, it's not gloom and doom. There is a Divine Plan in place, and we will all be high-fiving one another when we're on the other side of the veil after third-density. We will, once again, remember and be reunited with the One.

Chapter 25
The Life Purpose System

I have one more thing to set up here. It will help to tie up some loose ends of my twelve-inch journey. Maybe more importantly, it tells me a lot about exactly why I was drawn to music, performing, addiction, codependency, yoga, the Raelian Movement and, most of all, freedom.

This is for readers who are not familiar with *The Life Purpose System* by well known author Dan Millman, who also authored the acclaimed *Way of the Peaceful Warrior.*[39] This type of numerology is one of the first things that got my attention when visiting Toby for the first time, when I had not believed in any of it. Over these past couple of years, I have found this system to be very helpful in understanding myself. More than a few friends of mine were also quite surprised (and grateful) at how accurate it is in helping answer questions they had about themselves or loved ones.

Millman's system is built upon the idea that your soul had a specific plan in incarnating in your

---

[39] "About Dan Millman." The Peaceful Warrior's Way. https://www.peacefulwarrior.com/about-dan-millman-and-his-work/.

current life. We each come in here (physical) wanting to work on, or wanting to experience specific things, the pre-incarnate choices we all make before coming here. The soul contracts we have with others help us to "get our work done" here as well.

According to Dan Millman's Life Purpose System, something I would have laughed at only three years ago, we all choose what day we will be born because it does make a difference. My mother was in labor for seventy-two hours. It seems I really wanted to be born on June 21, 1958 on the summer solstice, and exactly at the time of day which puts me on the cusp's cusp. (Sorry to make you wait so long, Mom.)

Millman's system contains a set of three numbers. The first two add up to the third number on the right side of the slash, and this is one's main Life Purpose number. I have mentioned traits of my family several times in this book, and the numbers are a match every time. There are a ton of threes in our family. The three is about sensitivity and expression. My mother and all of her children are chock full of threes. It seems we are a sensitive bunch and that we need to express ourselves regularly. My mother is a thirty-three/six, one sister is a thirty-two/five, same as me, and Ann, is a thirty/three. The zero kind of amplifies the three, and she embodies this in every detail.

For example, I will break down my thirty-two/five.

- Three means that my soul wanted to work on sensitivity and expression.
- Two means I wanted to work on cooperation and balance.
- Five means I wanted to work on freedom and discipline.

Now, one can be "working their numbers" in the positive or in the negative – but we are all working our numbers one way or the other. For example, someone working their three (sensitivity and expression) in the positive will express themselves well, while someone working in the negative will be in the habit of criticizing or bad-mouthing. (Remember my mother criticizing my father in chapter two. She is thirty-three/six. To boot, the six has everything to do with acceptance and forgiveness.)

As I am now approaching sixty, I can look back and see how I was indeed working my numbers, sometimes in the negative, toward my main number, five. Sensitivity and expression (three) drew me to music, composing, teaching yoga, and things like this book. My three's sensitivity also drew me to wanting to numb myself from the denseness of our planet's current state. (Thus the drugs.) My two has led me through the lessons of cooperation and balance and has taken me longer to navigate. I laughed when I discovered an amusing joke that I played on myself in coming here. Twos make the best codependents, and Fives make the best dependents! Looking back at the drug addictions, I was obviously in a state of dependency. As much as my pride would like to not recognize it, I am still both of those. It is very clear to me that finding the RM when I did freed me (five) from the addictions of that time of my life. This launched me into a newfound freedom along with developing some great disciplines such as daily meditation, trying to serve humanity, composing music, yoga, and more.

Those working a five in their numbers also make good freedom fighters, and that is exactly what I was doing in the Raelian Movement. I had learned as a child that truth and justice were important to me, and I pursued it for almost twenty-three years in the Movement, fighting the good fight. Then, upon resigning from the RM, I gained an even deeper sense of freedom upon my "graduation."

About six months ago, I started wondering how many days I actually lived in KC over that time. I did the math in my head, and it seemed awfully close to 555. Knowing my main number is a five, I was thinking it would be interesting if that were the case. In the end, I couldn't quite get the math right because of the inclusive departure and return dates and leap year, so I Googled, "How many days between April 6, 2015 and October 17, 2016?" It came up as 560 days. So much for my idea. Then a few days later, I remembered that I had been on a five-day cruise ship gig with some Vegas friends. I couldn't help but see this as a cute little wink from the universe.

Chapter 26
Confirmations and Connections

This book has contained stories of protection and guidance. Higher Self has protected me many times, sometimes even from myself. Had They not intervened in Dallas, I would still have been in prison to this day (or even dead) after the incident with the police. And I can't help but believe I missed their message when my guitar was stolen in 1984 and the haunting "scar guitar" would find its way into my hands. Had I been able to interpret the message, would I have become more aware of the spiritual war taking place referred to in the reference to Revelations 20:10 on the guitar? Then there were the other times I was able to hear the Voice, like when I was told to go to the Mandalay Bay hotel to start looking for work, and thirty minutes later I landed the best gig I ever had, lasting almost ten years. Another big milestone was when I was able to hear the Voice telling me that my time in the RM was complete. And though it took a couple of years for me to hear it, the one that made me squirm the most was the Voice's clarion call to go back to KC. If not for the fourteen months there, I would not have experienced the immense freedom when the Voice reassured me that the karma I was to clear up in the Midwest was complete. The list of confirmations continues to grow, and the Voice (I call it my wife now) guides me well.

As Toby told me before I could understand, "they" used my aging parents to get me to KC so that I could work through karma. This was long term karma from a couple of thousand years ago and had largely to do with Nina telling me that I was one of Yeshua's disciples. (As well as Grace exclaiming, "That's why you're here! All of His disciples are being called back to this area." This was referring to the *Heart of the Dove* in the book *The Keys of Enoch*.) Then three months later, Kim confirmed this when I asked her what the karma was, and she told me it was about an energy exchange and more specifically, I was downloading energy from the area. Kim also told me at the time that I was supposed to create something upon returning to Vegas. They have been telling me for a year that I am to write this book as well as co-found the beloved meditation group we had in Las Vegas, which was a safe haven for all things fringe as well as meditating on STO vibrations for the world. I now wonder what else They continue to tell me from the other side of the veil. But I can tell you. I am now listening!

I also burned through short-term karma while in KC in facing who I was in 1983. I now understand that it wasn't Ricky wanting to escape KC. It was the fact that I wanted to escape the denseness of the planet itself that felt so foreign to me. And like any Wanderer who starts to remember on some level that they want to be in service to humanity, I resonated with the RM. I remembered "life out there" and that earth was in need of love, compassion, peace, and equality. And the good fight would eventually help me to remember that even good fights perpetuate separation.

I now understand that, karmically speaking, in running from anything, we are only postponing the lesson. The lesson will always come back to us – until we learn it. I absolutely had to go back to KC and face the person this forgetful Wanderer was in those decades. While 2012 – 2016 would be increasingly uncomfortable, things finally became blissfully rewarding as I started to remember: My Higher Self chose to come here. Once I got that, it was my great honor to be here. I truly do not believe that things could have turned out any better than they have. In fact, I believe it was inevitable that these things would happen. It was just a matter of which timeline they would happen on.

Most of all, I believe I have an idea of what the Divine Grace is which Kahotep told me I would soon be connected to. (As much as a third-density guy can have, anyway) Through the karmic balancing mentioned, I was finally able to connect with self-forgiveness. Like many of us, I was always quick to forgive others. I learned that lesson when I was eight. But I now have a great prize; Self-forgiveness. I saved for last what I consider to be Ra's most powerful teaching. This lesson is echoed precisely in *A Course In Miracles* as well as many of Dolores Cannon's workings.

34.4 Questioner: ...Would you define karma?

Ra: I am Ra. Our understanding of karma is that which may be called inertia. Those actions which are put into motion will continue using the ways of balancing until such time as the controlling or higher principle which you may liken unto your braking or stopping is invoked. This stoppage of the inertia of action may be called forgiveness. These two concepts are inseparable.

34.5 Questioner: If an entity develops what is called a karma in an incarnation, is there then programming that sometimes occurs so that he will experience catalyst that will enable him to get to a point of forgiveness thereby alleviating the karma?

Ra: I am Ra. This is, in general, correct. However, both self and any involved other-self may, at any time through the process of understanding, acceptance, and forgiveness, ameliorate these patterns. This is true at any point in an incarnative pattern. Thus one who has set in motion an action may forgive itself and never again make that error. This also brakes or stops what you call karma.

Etymologically speaking, most sources state that the meaning of the word "repentance" means "to see things in a different way," or "to change one's mind." This would be perfectly in line with Jesus' teachings that forgiveness and repentance are always related.

From a different session:

18.12 Questioner: You stated yesterday that forgiveness is the eradicator of karma. I am assuming that balanced forgiveness for the full eradication of karma would require forgiveness not only of other-selves but forgiveness of self. Am I correct?

Ra: I am Ra. You are correct. We will briefly expand upon this understanding in order to clarify. Forgiveness of other-self is forgiveness of self. An understanding of this insists upon full forgiveness upon the conscious level of self and other-self, for they are one. A full forgiveness is thus impossible without the inclusion of self.

In plainest terms, in forgiveness lies the end of karma. When I realized this, I remembered, as Toby had told me, more at one time than any time before. This sentence is a mantra of mine, and I sometimes reflect, gratefully, on learning so much about forgiveness when I understood: There is nothing to forgive.

Yoga teaches a concept called tapas, which invites to recognize and choose a more challenging path of discipline in order to burn off impurities we are carrying. It derives from the Sanskrit word *tap* (which means heat) and to put it in other terms, one might call it the proverbial baptism of fire. My initiation took me about four years, and the hottest part was the first fourteen months in KC in order to traverse a little further on the twelve-inch journey. Tapas was the gift that has placed me in grace and self-forgiveness.

I have one final yoga reference for you. The *kleshas* in yoga give the five causes of all pain and suffering a person can experience. The first one is ignorance, meaning that we have forgotten who we are. When we identify with our mind and body, we have forgotten who we are, and we identify with the second of the kleshas, egoism. In other words, we are in our heads, not our hearts. Thanks to the twelve-inch journey, I am remembering.

So be well my fellow Wanderers, Star Seeds, co-creators and spiritual seekers! Go! Continue to take in all the experiences you possibly can in order to return with your unique prize for the one infinite Creator. I am reminded of this quote from Rumi.

> You've no idea how hard I've looked for
> a gift to bring you. Nothing seems right.
> What's the point of bringing gold to the
> gold mine, or water to the ocean.
> Everything I came up with was like
> taking spices to the Orient. It's no good
> giving my heart and my soul because
> you already have these. So, I brought
> you a mirror. Look at yourself and
> remember me.

Chapter 27
Conclusion

Writing this book has been therapeutic, and my faithful assistant, Freddy the cat, has given me countless breaks I mentioned in the Introduction. (Seriously, at least 100 of them.) I recently ran across something that seemed quite fitting as we close. It's known as *The Hymn of the Pearl,* and it is a Gnostic text found in the gospel of Thomas.[40]

It tells of a boy from a high royal family who was the son of the highest of kings. His father sends him to Egypt to retrieve a pearl from a serpent. He soon forgets his mission, having been seduced by the Egyptians' culture. His father, the king of kings, sends him a letter and reminds him of his past, or his true origin. Upon remembering, the son retrieves the pearl and returns home.

I deeply resonate with this story as I feel this is what happened to me. In fact, I now believe it happens to many of us. We all forget thanks to the veil, some more or less than others. I received the call from the Voice on the other side of the veil, akin to the letter in this story, and I started to remember. I did not

---

[40] "The Hymn of the Pearl - The Acts of Thomas." The Gnostic Society Library. http://gnosis.org/library/hymnpearl.htm.

understand the call when I first received it. But soul contracts like Toby, Grace, and others put me back on course. My mission might seem to have been delayed by almost twenty-three years having denied all forms of Divinity. But I do not see it that way. I believe, now, that it was actually my Higher Self's plan all along to deny Source, God, Creator. How would it feel to disconnect completely from Spirit? What adventure might await? What part in the Divine Plan might be experienced? It was a risky move for this Wanderer. Because what if I hadn't remembered? But thanks to my remembering, the rewards were all the sweeter for it. As I started to remember, *The Hymn of the Pearl* became something real and not just a mythic, poetic tale.

There is a word which, like several words in our modern world, could be considered overused. Words like love or awesome are tossed about so often that they have been diluted. They have lost their original power, their true meanings. One such word is namaste. Yoga tradition invites one to recognize that there is a Divine spark within each of us. That Divine spark is one of an infinite number of Divine sparks which originally came from the one infinite Creator. (Not unlike the Law of One.) The Divine spark would also be how most of us define the word soul. This spark is said to reside in one's heart chakra. We could call this the seat of the soul. Since the heart is the first organ created in a foetus, this is not a stretch of our imagination. In so many words, namaste is a way of saying "the divine spark in me acknowledges the divine spark in you." I didn't believe any of this five years ago. I only believe it now because of what happened to me. If there is one thing you take from this book, I hope that it is *in forgiveness lies the end of karma.*

Namaste.

Favorite Sources of Information

llresearch
Carla Rueckert
Dolores Cannon
David Wilcock
David Icke
Michael Tellinger
Edgar Cayce
Colin Joe Byrne
Anodea Judith (On Chakras)
Dr. Judy Wood (On the 9/11 buildings collapsing)
Dr. Michael Newton
Toby Evans
William Tompkins
Corey Goode
Dr. Michael Salla
Dr. Pete Peterson

Jim Marrs
William Bramley
Simon Parkes
Graham Hancock
Emery Smith
The Yoga Sutras by Sri Swami Satchidananda
Ra

Made in the USA
Columbia, SC
01 November 2019

82559382R00131